THE LIFE AND SELECTED WRITINGS OF

ST. BULUS AL - BUSHI

BISHOP OF CAIRO AND ITS DISTRICTS

THE LIFE AND SELECTED WRITINGS OF

ST. BULUS AL- BUSHI

BISHOP OF CAIRO AND ITS DISTRICTS

ST SHENOUDA PRESS
SYDNEY, AUSTRALIA
2024

The Life and Selected Writings of St Bulus Al-Bushi
Bishop of Cairo and its Districts

COPYRIGHT © 2024
Second Revised Edition
St. Shenouda Press

All rights reserved. Except for brief quotations in critical publications or reviews, no part of this book may be reproduced in any manner without prior written permission from the publisher.

ST SHENOUDA PRESS
8419 Putty Rd,
Putty, NSW, 2330
Sydney, Australia

www.stshenoudapress.com

ISBN 13: 978-0-6455543-9-7

Cover Design:
Dionysia Tanios
@dionysiandesigns

All scripture quotations, unless otherwise indicated, are taken from the New King James Version®. Copyright © 1982 by Thomas Nelson, Inc. Used by permission. All rights reserved.

TABLE OF CONTENTS

Publisher's Introduction 7

Section I The Life of St Bulus Al-Bushi

The Life of St Bulus Al-Bushi 11

Section II Selected Writings

I Feast of the Annunciation 55

II Glorious Nativity 71

III Glorious Epiphany 91

IV Palm Sunday 107

V Crucifixion 117

VI Holy Resurrection 147

VII The Feast of the Ascension 173

VIII The Feast of Pentecost 185

PUBLISHER'S INTRODUCTION

St Bulus al-Bushi has and will be known as one of the greatest theologians in the history of the Coptic Middle Ages. His extensive contributions to writing in Arabic had extensive effects to Egyptian Christians and other groups as he was one of the first authors to write in the Arabic language rather than translate from the Greek or Coptic as was common at the time.

He was probably born between 1170 and 1175 and was a native of the city of Bush north of Bani Suef in Middle Egypt. His lifespan was closely paralleled to the Ayyubid rule in Egypt (1171-1250) and passed away around 1250. He joined the monastery of Anba Samuel of Qalamun in the Fayyum province. His fame greatly increased when he was one of three monks nominated to succeed John Pope VI (who died in 1216) as patriarch of Alexandria, though he withdraw his nomination. During the last decade of his life, he was ordained as the first bishop of Cairo.

The eight homilies translated in this book are arguably his most famous work which are attested to in dozens of manuscripts. These homilies were given on the major church feasts. Traditionally they homely on Good Friday is read at the sixth hour of Good Friday in the Coptic Orthodox church. These homilies are characterised by their extensive use of scripture, as well as his ability to integrate theological and spiritual themes, which puts him in line with the great church fathers of the fourth and fifth centuries.

Section I

The Life of St Bulus Al-Bushi

St Bulus Al-Bushi
Bishop of Cairo and its Districts

By: Father Jacob Moyzer

"Nor do they light a lamp and put it under a basket, but on a lampstand, and it gives light to all who are in the house."
Matthew 5:15

Seven centuries ago, the Coptic Church was suffering in various ways from both within and without. An era where its spiritual condition deteriorated due to the mismanagement of its leaders, it became unstable, its business came to a halt and, due to some embarrassing and disgraceful incidents, the solidarity between its members was shattered. A time when the Coptic people were divided into many factions in the worst possible way, to the extent of bloodshed, and its guides could not maintain peace or unity and were unable to come to an agreement concerning the most suitable candidate to be appointed to the patriarchal see leaving it vacant for nineteen years at one time. An age when it was known that the priests could not discern the honour of their rank so that even confessions heard were no longer confidential, forcing Abba Yoannis VI, 74th patriarch of Alexandria (1189 – 1216) to suspend the reception of the sacrament of confession;

At that time, there appeared a serene man, a lover of his people, who was detached from factional passions, not concerned with any matter apart from promoting the church and advancing its status. A venerable scholar with extensive knowledge in religion given to study and scrutiny of complex religious and moral problems affecting his troubled times. A priest whose heart was inflamed by the zeal of the Apostle Paul, a capable interpreter of and commentator on divine scripture, a revealer of its mysteries and elaborator of its ambiguities. An eloquent religious orator who raised up and kindled averse hearts, a driven, intellectual and skilled debater with powerful arguments resembling the five smooth stones in David's pouch with which he contested Goliath the Philistine, and hurled with great skill injuring and striking down his feeble opponent. A truly honourable bishop, guiding and guarding the physical and spiritual wellbeing of his congregation – St Bulus al-Bushi[1], Bishop of Misr.[2]

Can he be counted as one of the Copts' most eminent and insightful leaders? Should today's Copts be proud of his achievements? Should they take up his writing and look to his character as a lamp to depart from the present darkness of divisiveness into the light of solidarity, cooperation and unity? Would Copts, whether priests, bishops, or secular leaders, do well to emulate his admirable example and to walk in his footsteps, especially considering that evidence of division and signs of discord have begun to appear in a regrettable manner? Here, we would like to answer these questions honestly. It is therefore necessary for us, in these pages, to reveal the significant standing of this venerable bishop and his distinguished status among his contemporaries. We will also show why it is right for us to include him in the rank of those great Copts who have served their church and nation in critical circumstances despite

---

1 He is thus called because of his attention to his township Boush (Governate of Bani Suef) see *E. Amélineau, La géographie de l'Egypte à l'époque copte (Paris, 1893), pp 369-370 and Basha Mubarak, The New Plans for Egypt and Misr (Cairo 1305), pp 5-6*

2 The reader who wishes to know specific information about this diocese from the beginning to the 20th century may consult the valuable articles published by Kamel Saleh Nakhla in the *Sehyon (Zion) Journal* 1947-1949 entitled T*he Diocese of Misr* and *The Bishopric of Misr*. It saddens us that, in his research, he never mentions St Bulus al-Bushi who has become one of this see's most important and famous bishops in the history of the Coptic Church. We also do not agree with his assertion that, *"the name of the bishop of Misr disappeared from the pages of history in the 13th century,"* (Refer to Sehyon (Zion) Journal (1665 AM 1949 AD Vol 2 February) p39), since in 1240, the Synod appointed St Bulus al-Bushi Bishop of Misr assistant to and overseer over Pope Kyrillos Ibn Laqlaq. Perhaps he meant *"after the 13th century"*. It would have been more beneficial in a historical sense had he published this research independently.

the insufficient information imparted about him by historical sources.

Perhaps this is one of the reasons that caused present-day church historians favourably mention3 him, and why he never received due consideration and recognition in their writings. If we fulfil this, we will have performed our duty and done justice to a great man who had been overlooked by historians, along with his virtue and high standing. This omission was probably due to a wish by historians to avoid citing details of some embarrassing and atrocious incidents that occurred during the patriarchate of Pope Kyrillos Ebn Laqlaq and so have covered them up. Nothing demonstrated this more than **The History of the Patriarchs of the Church of Alexandria,** which included only a few lines describing the period lasting twenty-seven years.

We, however, aspire to place the glowing light of his life atop a lampstand, not under a basket, that it may shine on every Copt who loves the history of his fathers and who is proud of their influence. This personality attracted my attention during my research on famous Copts of the 12th and 13th centuries. It appealed to my interest and compelled me to delve into various historical sources desiring to discover as much as possible about his life, his writing, the depths of his merits and the importance of his accomplishments. When the administration of the Society of Mari Mena in Alexandria invited me to write about a famous and brilliant Copt, I realised that this was my opportunity to portray the life of St Bulus al-Bushi, from a historical perspective. I wanted to do this before the readers of this "letter", issued by the Society, and to reiterate the words of the Holy Gospel, **"A city that is set on a hill cannot be hidden.**[4]

---

3 Refer to **The History of the Coptic Nation collated by ElFakir Elayhe Taala Yacoub Nakhla Rofeela, 1**[st] Edition, Cairo, 1898 pp 183-203
4 Matthew 5:14

We will first mention the most important incidents of his life, and then we will see how he illuminated his generation and became renowned in his day as a theologian, an interpreter of scripture, a debater and a ecclesiastical orator. The sources could not provide any information on the first two stages of his life – his life as a youth and as a layman – and the last in which he became secluded in one of the monasteries. Though I could not find a direct declaration in any of the references, it may be assumed that he was a monk at the monastery of El Fayoum based on two facts. Firstly, his birthplace Boush[5] is located in the north of middle Egypt not far from the district of El Fayoum, which was populated at that time by monasteries. Secondly the friendship that bound him throughout his life to Kyrillos Ebn Laqlaq, who was a known monk in the Monastery of El Fayoum. Therefore, St Bulus al-Bushi was very likely also a monk at the same time and at the same monastery. It is likely, also, that he was ordained a priest in the same monastery to which he belonged as per the custom followed by monasteries from that time on.

On 7th January, 1216 AD, Pope Yoannis VI, 74th patriarch of Alexandria departed. This was at the beginning of the century known in the history of the Coptic Church for its violent disputes around who would be fitting for the patriarchal see. There is no doubt that, whoever reads the history of the leadership of this patriarch, could clearly see that the atmosphere in the church at the time was bleak, and that there were signs boding a severe crisis for the church due to the division of its bishops and the religious decadence of both the clergy and the laity. Rather than the community uniting its opinion by electing a person known for his piety and knowledge, it revealed a repulsive guise by forming three diverse factions waging war against each other. Here, for

---

5 He was called al-Bushi

the first time on the pages of history, we hear the name **Bulus al-Bushi** as a candidate to the patriarchal see. The name of the priest Daoudd Ebn Laqlaq also appears as another candidate who successfully attained the patriarchal see. There was a third strong contender no less passionate about his accession to the see than the priest Daoudd, who resorted to illicit means to attain his desire to satisfy his greed. He was the Archdeacon Abu Shaker Botros who was superintendent of the Church of Saints Sergius and Bacchus in Kasr El Shama[6].

There is no opportunity here to narrate the details of these battles and their motives that are devoid of the spirit of reason and religion. All those who went down to the battlefield, rather than relying on convincing their adversaries through proofs, principles and the reforms they sought, they relied instead on counterfeit weapons such as betrayal, defamation, rebellion and protests at the doors of the churches. I will summarise the situation as follows: Each of the three factions exerted every effort to have its candidate appointed, and for a long time fought the others aggressively without yielding and without resolution. It would appear to any historian that a fierce election battle was being fought over a secular position rather than over the selection of the chief religious leader.

It is known about the faction of Abu Shaker Botros that it had used unlawful tactics including tendering a vast sum of money, reported to be around three thousand gold dinars, to the treasury in exchange for the patriarchal position, this was beside the huge sums it offered to the Sultan ElAdel. These disputes and quarrels caused the atmosphere in the church to become gloomy, and despite all these efforts, the patriarchal see remained unoccupied for a period of nineteen years and five months. Throughout this time, the Coptic Church was exposed

---

6 This is the Fort of Babylon in Old Cairo containing many historical churches.

to such anarchy that it crippled all its services. Also during this time, all of its bishops except two departed so that when Kyrillos Ebn Laqlaq illegitimately became patriarch in 1325, they were the only two bishops to consecrate him. This event was recorded in the history of the church as a rare occurrence. It may be noted here that, despite the intensity of the conflict between the factions and the quarrels that almost resulted in the shedding of blood, Bulus al-Bushi and Kyrillos Ibn Laqlaq remained companions and were never separated, collaborating and cooperating in authoring books in defence of the principles and the dignity of the Christian faith.

It is worthwhile to note that throughout this time, Kyrillos Ibn Laqlaq did not miss an opportunity to achieve his goal of the patriarchal office by any means, while his friend the priest Bulus al-Bushi did not leave him alone in the realm of research and writing. From this we can deduce that, after seeing that the tensions around the patriarchal title had reached its peak, and that the position itself had taken on a form a man eager for godliness and piety would abhor, the latter turned aside from this ambition. He contentedly and honourably pulled out of this battlefield choosing to devote himself to religious research in a quiet atmosphere, and to continue to spread divine truths by any means - pen, sermon, guidance or response to anyone bent on discrediting the Christian faith. Indeed this is the conduct of superior men and the way of noble ones and in this is sure proof of the sobriety of his mind, the gentleness of his character, the temperance of his habits and his great love for preserving the good of the church and the security of the Coptic people.

Rather than wade through the upheaval of rebellion and vilification, and fearing that the clarity of his spiritual life would be soiled by plunging into a worldly current, or by resorting to disreputable means of gaining personal goals and causing offense to the honour of his priesthood, he preferred instead a quiet life to a troubled one and a tranquil life to a restless one, thereby becoming the victor. Through his voluntary withdrawal, he opened the way for his friend Daoudd Ibn Laqlaq who did not spare any effort with ElSheikh Abu Fatouh to obtain an order from the king for his appointment as patriarch whether by trickery, deception and bribery or by force and terror against the bishops. Finally, he obtained what he desired and took the patriarchal office through the power of the governing authorities on 7th January, 1235. Consequently, the church experienced adversity and scandal previously unheard of, and history has denigrated his life to the point that it has been recorded with extreme brevity. Here is what was recorded in **THE HISTORY OF THE PATRIARCHS OF ALEXANDRIA**[7] about his life:

Kyrillos the seventy-fifth Patriarch of the order

This father Kyrillos Ibn Laqlaq was consecrated at the city of Alexandria on Sunday, the twenty-second of the month of Bau'unah in the year nine hundred and fifty-one of the Martyrs [1235 A.D.]. He remained patriarch for seven years and nine months, and he went to his rest on Tuesday, the fourteen of the month of Baramhat in the year nine hundred and fifty-nine of the Martyrs [1243 A.D.] at the Monastery of wax (El-Shamaa) at Gizah (al-Gizah), which he was buried in. He was a learned man and virtuous. He possessed a number of diverse virtues, except that he was a lover of money. He practised simony, and there befell him adversities on account of it. Some people withstood and despised him and held councils with regard to him in the presence of the viceroy (naib) of the Sultan and the arbiters (al-`Adul) and the wazir Ma`in ad-Din Ibn as-Sheikh, and they forced him to pay more than twelve thousand dinars. The throne

---

[7] G. Graf, Catalogue de manuscrits arabes chrétiens conservés au Caire (Studi e Testi 63), Città del Vaticano, 1934.

remained vacant after him for seven years and seven months. This father is he who drew up the Book of the Confession, the twenty-two sayings, and he called it the Book of the Teacher and the Disciple.[8]

It appears from this source that one of Abba Kyrillos' first undertakings after assuming the patriarchal see in 1235 was to consecrate his friend Bulus al-Bushi bishop over Misr and its services. At the beginning, he also consecrated another eleven bishops, since at that time there remained only two bishops in Egypt due to the departure of all other bishops during the twenty-nine years the see of Alexandria remained unoccupied. One of the most famous of these bishops was Abba Christodoulos metropolitan of Damietta[9], Yusab bishop of Fuwwah[10], author of **THE HISTORY OF THE PATRIARCHS OF ALEXANDRIA**, *and Yoannis bishop of Samannud*[11]. Unfortunately, we do not know exactly when the consecration of St Bulus was. Kyrillos ibn Laqlaq did not accomplish all that his supporters had hoped he would accomplish; due to his great love for money as well as the terror and cruelty he inflicted in order to attain his goals. In the fifth year of his patriarchate, when the bishops saw the situation was becoming more complex and adverse due to his eccentric behaviour, they convened a synod in September 1240 AD (Tute 957 AM) in the Citadel before the Wazir (minister) Mu`ez ad-Din. The Synod issued eighteen canons reflecting decisive reform. One of these stipulates the appointment of *two scholarly bishops, one of whom is St Bulus al-Bushi Bishop*

---

8 History Of The Patriarchs Of The Egyptian Church By Sawirus Ibn Al-Mukaffa` Bishop Of Al-Ashmunin Volume iii. Part iii

9 Refer to his biography and works in G. Graf, Geschichte der christlichen arabischen Literatur. Città del Vaticano, Bibliotheca Apostolica Vaticana, 1944-1953. Vol 2 pp 378-379

10 Ibib., pp 369-371

11 Ibid., pp 371-375

of Misr, and the other a learned bishop of Lower Egypt, to attend the Patriarchal cell as official observers of the patriarch Kyrillos ibn Laqlaq[12], to put an end to his improper behaviour and to restrain his indulgent whims. Their high hopes were pinned particularly on the character of the prudent St Bulus al-Bushi to coax back, with his renowned wisdom, the matters of the patriarchate, and to remedy with firmness the faults of his old friend with his strong influence upon him.

St Bulus al-Bushi – a Noble Theological Scholar

St Bulus al-Bushi has left a number of valuable works still preserved in their entirety in manuscripts. Unfortunately, apart from his commentary on the last two chapters of the Book of Revelation and a sermon on the Feast of Theophany, none of his other works have been published. This is a sure indication of the lack of resolve of the educated class of the Coptic peoples to publish the legacy of their fathers and scholars, and of the lack of their passion to benefit from the same. If we mention this with much regret, we are not merely lamenting the fact that Copts have neglected the publication of the works of St Bulus al-Bushi, for this would be a minor neglect. The truth is that there are a large number of valuable works, authored by Copts, which for a long time have remained on the shelves of various Coptic libraries, whether in the Coptic Museum, historical churches, monasteries or the libraries of the Coptic Orthodox Patriarchate in Cairo and Alexandria, and which no one considered publishing. The years have passed and we

---

12   The reader may find all the sources of the manuscripts containing the text of these canons mentioned in G. Graf, Geschichte Vol ii p 364. These canons were published in a book of canons compiled by the elder alSafi ibn al-'Assal authored in 955 AM, reprinted (?) by Bishop Isidoros, Egypt 1927 AD (1644AM) Appendix p 31-35

have known our scholars by name only. We know the value of gold and silver but are ignorant of the value of our treasures that are more precious than gold and silver. These include, for example, the works of Abba Sawirus ibn al-Mukaffa, Abba Butros ElGamil bishop of Mallg, Rashid Abu el-Kheir ibn elTayeb, the sons of alAssal, Abba Mikhail bishop of Atrib and Mallg, Shams al-Riyasah Abu al-Barakat ibn Kabar and Butros alSadmanti, most of which has not been published to date. Some, who possess manuscripts, strive to keep them hidden as if averting envy or "the evil eye". If we now list what remains of the works of Coptic scholars who excelled in the thirteenth and fourteenth centuries that have not yet been published, we would fill tens of thousands of pages. We would be astonished, and finally realise our lamentable apathy regarding this work, and the precious time that has been wasted due to business in a stressful age and our rush toward futile animosity and conflict. We are lagging behind other denominations that have cared about the dissemination of its academic and religious heritage. Now that the number of Coptic societies are increasing at a steady rate appearing closely one after the other, and many of them work and strive without having unity or a leader; is it not time that a group of Coptic thinkers take on the establishment of one society that would embrace the publishing of those manuscripts that have accumulated on the shelves of Coptic libraries untouched even by the elite, and to preserve what has been deposited in these treasuries that are opened maybe only once a year? This is to say nothing of what we have seen with our own eyes of the damage caused to these treasures by humidity and moths, and still no one takes action to correct this sombre situation. I write in the margins of this article and repeat what the Roman senators directed at the consuls in ancient times, as perilous times loomed in the Roman Republic, **Caveant Consules.**

St Bulus al-Bushi showed laudable vigour in authoring works on various Christian subjects, particularly in those difficult days. These included books on systematic and moral theology, biblical exegesis, the science of religious rhetoric and the principles of dialectics. Here we will reveal some observations on the writings of St Bulus al-Bushi that have a direct connection to dogma or dogmatic theology.

St Bulus compiled a dissertation entitled **AN ARTICLE ON THE INTELLECTUAL PROOFS THAT BRINGS MAN TO THE KNOWLEDGE OF THE INCARNATE GOD**, that is the knowledge of the incarnate God intellectually. His intent for writing this research was to enable non-Christians to attain a knowledge of the Lord Christ, the incarnate God, and to reveal to them that the faith in the mystery of the incarnation, though beyond the intellect and the understanding, does not contradict, oppose or undervalue them at all but rather enhances, elevates and expands their scope. He would challenge them with rational, acceptable and authoritative proofs that were agreeable to the demands of the mind, until they expel from their thoughts false assertions and strip them of delusions, preparing before them the path to faith in Christ under the influence of divine grace.

By carrying out this research, he also wished to clarify Christian dogma, and in particular the mystery of the incarnation, to those outside the faith in a fashion acceptable to their minds so they are not subject to foolish objections. This allowed him to address the allegations of those who determine that Christian tenets are nothing more than a collection of fabled beliefs or the ideas of those who hold false philosophies. At the same time, his intention was to enhance the religious education of the Christians of his time and to establish their faiths in the Lord the Saviour.

This extensive research now may be found in a unique handwritten manuscript in the Bodleian Library, Oxford under number 38,5[13]. Unfortunately, we could not access it and, apparently, there is no other handwritten copy in Egypt, but know that until now we have not been able to enumerate all the Arabic Christian manuscripts in the land of Egypt. It is a possibility that this research, in a partial or abbreviated form, was kept at the Coptic Orthodox Patriarchate Library in Cairo in a handwritten manuscript, dating back to the fourteenth or fifteenth centuries, under the number 430,5 (Theology no. 600)[14]. This paper was entitled, *From a Religious Collection, compiled by St Bulus alBushi, bishop of Misr, entitled* **On the Incarnation** and this collection is comprised of twenty-one pages of which the last is missing. Here it would have been apt to come to you, the knowledgeable reader, with some of the details of the content of the book On the Incarnation, for that would have been a simple matter but we will not conceal from you that this library has not officially opened to scholars or to the public. We have a firm hope that, in the near future, it will open its doors to those who are concerned with research into the timeless Christian antiquities, so that we may return to the reader with another research comparing On the Incarnation with other volumes of the same title written by other Coptic academics that excelled in the 13th century. To this we add that it is very possible that the contents of this copy is part of what is found in manuscript number 224 from page 61 to page 235 inclusive (1705 AD) described by Cardinal Eugene Tisserant in the index of the Arabic manuscripts in the Borgia Arabic collection as follows:

---

13 J. Uri, Bibliothecase Bodleianae codd. Mss.Orientalium catalogus. P. I. (Oxonu, 1787), ms. 38,5.
14 Refer to G. Graf. Catalogue, p 157 ms. 430,5 foll. 98 r-119r.

Conlectio dictorum ss. Patrum de Trinitate, Incarnatione. Etc auctore Anba Paulo al-Busi[15]

We should also mention that St Bulus authored another work entitled, THE BOOK OF THE SPIRITUAL SCIENCES of which, as far as I could determine, there is only one handwritten copy in the library of the Syrian Monastery in Wadi el Natrun no 37/4 comprising 347 pages (24-25 lines, measuring 30cmx22cm) and dated 1576 AM[16]. Unfortunately none of the esteemed fathers, the monks of that monastery, have until now attended to this rare manuscript to provide the Coptic people with an article about the importance of its contents and rarity.

Our intention in writing this article, then, is to light the way before the reader and to familiarise him with the works of St Bulus that he may appreciate the magnitude of the effort he exerted in propagating religious truths and in reviving and strengthening the spirit of true Christian ethics amongst the children of faith. We should not ignore, also, what he has offered in great support and practical partnership to Abba Kyrillos Ebn Laqlaq in producing a considerable work to treat an essential Christian discipline entitled THE BOOK OF CONFESSION, also known as THE BOOK OF THE TEACHER AND THE DISCIPLE.

The scholar al-Asad Abu al-Farag Hibat Allah Ebn al-Assal wrote a valuable preface to this book in which he mentioned that the two translated into Arabic all that existed in the Coptic language regarding the Mystery of Confession in the writings of the holy fathers annotating it with a complete explanation. Al-Asad also mentions that he had helped them in organising the

---

15 Eugene Tisserant, Inventaire Sommaire des mss. arabes du fonds Borgia à la Bibliothèque Vaticane (Estratto dalla Miscellanea Fr. Ehrle V., Roma, 1924 p 21, ms.224,ff 6/r-235

16 This information is derived from a catalogue compiled by Yassa Abd al-Masih of yet unpublished manuscripts found in historical Egyptian churches and monasteries that are kept by him.

subject matter of this work, and had cooperated with them in refining the Arabic expressions. This valuable book, copious in its subject matter, solid in its teachings, sublime in its spirituality, was compiled by Kyrillos Ebn Laqlaq before his ascension to the patriarchal see (1235 AD) in association with St Bulus, who was at the time a priest. The aim of them writing this book, was to return the Sacrament of Confession its critical and sublime status amongst the seven sacraments of the church, so that the faithful do not remain deprived of its spiritual benefits after Abba Yoannis VI, 74th patriarch of Alexandria (1189 – 1216) had temporarily suspended its use due to the clergy's lack of reverence for it and the decadence of their morals, as previously stated. This book then came along revealing and proving, with irrefutable proofs and convincing arguments, the necessity of the repentant sinner's recourse to this mystery as a legitimate means, commanded by the Lord of the church, for the washing of a conscience sullied by sin. It is likened to the Pool of Siloam, and is positioned as an only door to sincere repentance, attainment of forgiveness and rest for the conscience.

We should mention, too, that this book is rife with extensive explanation to guide a conscience tarnished with transgression and to save it from slavery to sin through admission, regret, weeping, atonement, spiritual reform and the refinement of morals. This book, then, is worthy to be referred to as the book of spiritual medicine. Notably, despite there being many handwritten copies of this book in the libraries of all the monasteries as well as in the library of The Coptic Museum, a matter that demonstrates its merits and its importance amongst the different Coptic circles, it has not yet been published. How commendable it would be if a Coptic society, devoted to the writings of the fathers, published it, copying it faithfully though not literally, so that the Coptic people may consider the truth of the Mystery of Confession, its traditions, characteristics and its

The life of St Bulus Al-Bushi

important spiritual benefits[17] and the importance of its practice, especially in these days. Regrettably, Copts both young and old, have neglected it. Many have mistakenly become content with prayer and fasting as a means of receiving forgiveness of sins, and parted from the sacrament of Confession.

For the benefit of those who wish to acquaint themselves with this author, we will point out that there are a number of handwritten manuscripts in the Coptic Museum, three of which are: a) Manuscript 123 (Theology 209) comprised of 23 discourses[18,] 220 pages long, dating back to the 17th century; b) Manuscript 129 (Theology 215) comprised of 22 discourses, 136 pages long, dating back to the same time; c) Manuscript 131 (Theology 217)[19] comprised of 22 discourses, 244 pages long, the first discourse missing its first page, dating back to the 14th century[20]. Due to the importance of this book and its prominence, I find it appropriate to copy here for the reader as an example from this author, a page of the Manuscript 131 (Theology 217) from the Coptic Museum[21], page 15 v to 16 v. The reader will notice that the book takes the form of a dialogue between a disciple and a teacher, meaning that the disciple poses questions to the teacher about how the penitent can be delivered from his sins and about the necessity of the confession

---

17 This book mentions ten benefits to the mystery of Confession.
18 Called "Door" or "Obelisk" (or Subject) in some copies.
19 This copy may have been with the incomplete Manuscript 113 (Theology 199), one of the oldest existing copies
20 Refer to G. Graf, Catalogue, pp 49,52, ms. 131 as well as Murqus Simaykah Pasha and Yassa Abd al-Massih, CATALOGUE OF THE COPTIC AND ARABIC MANUSCRIPTS IN THE COPTIC MUSEUM, THE PATRIARCHATE, THE PRINCIPAL CHURCHES IN CAIRO AND ALEXANDRIA, AND THE MONASTERIES OF EGYPT VOLUME 1, Cairo, 1939-1942 pp 27, 36 and 37.
21 This manuscript dates back to the 14th century and is the oldest handwritten copy of THE BOOK OF THE TEACHER AND THE DISCIPLE in the Coptic Museum, copied around one hundred years after it was written.

of offences. We see that the disciple through his questions, and the teacher through his answers, seek inspiration in the events mentioned in the Old Testament, in the sayings of the Lord Christ and in the parables he uttered in the four gospels pointing to the sacrament of Confession.

From the first question:

> **15 v. The disciple said,** "And where else does He command us to confess besides in the Holy Gospel. **The teacher said,** "John the Apostle, in the first chapter of his first epistle, calls the concealment of sin darkness and its confession light, and says that if we conceal it then we alone have overshadowe[22] ourselves and do not accomplish the truth. If we confess it then the Lord is just and faithful to forgive us our sins and to cleanse us from all unrighteousness[23]. **The disciple said,** "And what is the meaning of his saying, 'If we confess it then the Lord is just and faithful to forgive our sins'? What is the meaning of his saying 'the Lord is just and faithful'?" **The teacher said,** "It is He who made the just promise that whoever confesses his sins[24] He would forgive them." **The disciple said,** "And where did He promise this? Do you see Him making His promise through the words of John the Baptist?" **The teacher said,** "And through the words of those other than John the Baptist in 15 r. countless places. In the Holy Gospel He says that there is nothing covered that will not be cleansed[25], nor hidden that will not be known and that whatever you speak in the dark will be heard in the light. He called concealment darkness. He says that whatever you do in the dark, meaning in secret, will be heard in the light, meaning I will reveal it and expose you

---

22 Read 'deceived'.
23 The First Epistle of Saint John 1:8-9
24 This word is not accented in this copy.
25 Read 'revealed'.

through it, on the day of light, the day on which the secrets of the hearts will appear, as the Apostle says. Each person will be known for what he does in secret[26] and will be exposed and humiliated before all the angels, humans and demons, for the words of the Lord are truth and not one of[27] His words can be contradicted for Heaven and earth will pass away, but His words will not pass away28. He said that there is nothing covered that will not be revealed, for all that man has done in secret in this world will surely be cleansed[29], and He will expose him through it. For this reason He, to whom be the glory, has commanded each one of us to confess his sins to his priest, who is only one person, and to declare to him what was in secret and to accomplish the word of the Lord which must be accomplished, and so is His saying that there is nothing covered that will not be revealed. If he accomplishes it in this way, and reveals the hidden, the Lord will not do it again 16 v. and will not expose him once more, for it has been accomplished and completed. So, by baring oneself to one other person and through this beneficial exposure and gentle humiliation he is spared and is saved from an unbeneficial exposure and an uncomfortable humiliation before all of creation. This is His faithful promise in which He promised that whoever confesses his sins and reveals it to another seeking salvation, it will be forgiven him and it will not be exposed[30] once more, and for his sake Saint John said that whoever confesses his sins, the Lord is just and faithful to forgive him his sins and to cleanse him from all unrighteousness31. He called the concealment of sin, in this place, darkness

---

26 Saint Paul's First Epistle to the Corinthians 3:13
27 The word 'of' is crossed out.
28 Matthew 24:35.
29 Read 'revealed'.
30 Meaning: God will not expose it.
31 Copied as is written

and its revelation light as the Lord had done in the other place ..."[32]

Apparently, the **BOOK OF THE TEACHER AND THE DISCIPLE** is abridged from another book with the title **KITAB AL-RU'US** or the **BOOK OF HEADINGS** written at the beginning of the 12th century by an unknown author. The writer of this book, comprised of 33 'headings'[33], deals with the obligation of the layman generally and of the monk, the hermit and the recluse specifically, to take for himself "a spiritual teacher" or "a spiritual physician, that he may walk according to the divine laws for the continuance of his steadfastness in love, the life of virtue, the attainment of perfection, the preservation of his soul from the temptation and deception of Satan and the vigilance against evil thoughts, and especially for the attainment of eternal salvation, and to also confess his offences at the hands of his 'teacher'". A footnote in a handwritten copy[34] of the **BOOK OF CONFESSION** or the **BOOK OF THE TEACHER AND THE DISCIPLE** by Abba Kyrillos Ebn Laqlaq kept in the Syrian Library at the Sharfa Monastery, supports this quote as follows: *"The Book of Confession, also called the Book of the Teacher and the Disciple, is almost a summary of the Book of headings and includes its [Book of headings] most appealing and important topics."*[35]

Before I conclude speaking about the theological research St Bulus had devoted himself to carrying out, I must finally mention that he had expressed his valuable opinion regarding a problem many Coptic scholars in particular, and oriental scholars in general, from the 10th to the 14th centuries, had studied from several perspectives and had expressed an opinion

---

32 Copied as is written
33 Meaning 'chapters'
34 Written in Garshuni alphabet. Syrian number 49 dated 1726 AD.
35 Refer to G. Graf, Geschichte der christlichen arabischen literature, Bd. II (Città del Vaticano, 1947), p. 368-369

on. A problem that was a "current" problem at the time, and which had drawn the attention of many researchers to the issue. This issue may be summarised by determining what falls within the scope of human actions such as walking, talking, the various occupations, prayer, fasting, all that befalls man of both good and evil; from an inevitable situation or from a judgement by the Almighty God, and whatever remains for man after this, of choice in his actions and in the planning of the affairs of his life. From of old[36], this problem has been called the problem of "Predestination".

It may be noted that this brief expression has its meaning and special interpretation in the Christian religion, as it does in some other religions and philosophical schools of thought. It is, undoubtedly, a vital problem and has a deep and direct impact on the whole human being, inwardly and outwardly, and enters not only into the depths of his actions, but also into the reservoirs of his instincts, inclinations, longings and feelings. In accordance with how a man solves this problem, whether in the light of abstract reasoning or religious requirements, he will direct himself to live in line with this solution and to anticipate happiness or misery in the afterlife. There is no rational man who does not stand before it wondering with great concern. How can they not wonder? I wonder – am I compelled or free to choose what I do as a human being? Am I under the judgement of predestination, or do I have some portion, small or large, in directing my life morally and materially? Will He, who created me without my will, one day, save me without my will? Are livelihoods as well as lifespans with all their spiritual, mental and physical afflictions, defined, so that all I can do is to stand idly before all these judgements like a deaf machine, walking and moving under the influence and power of a compelling

---

36 Refer to the teachings of Mani.

hand? And, if both the good and the bad are submissive to the judgement of predestination, as a fixed system governing them, then what would bring me to trust in the Almighty God and what would be the benefit of that trust? I cannot here explore the depths of this complex question with the reader but I will be content to present some of what Coptic scholars had written before St Bulus had thrown this question upon the carpet of research.

Abu al-Barakat ibn Kabar, in his book **MISBAH AL-ZULMAH, FIIDAH AL-KHIDMAH**[37] (The Luminary of Church Services), mentions in the midst of the works of Sawirus ibn al-Muqaffa his work entitles **NAZM AL-JAWHAR WA-L-DURAR, FI L-RADD ALA L-QAWL BI-L-QADA WA-L-QADAR** (Stringing together of Jewel and Pearls, in answer to the doctrine of fate and divine decree)[38]. Till this day, a handwritten copy of it has not emerged in any of the libraries, except possibly a handwritten manuscript of the same title, including an answer to the teaching of predestination, may be found in the Oriental Library in Beirut, no 589, comprised of 233 pages, dated from the 16th century but is attributed to al-Shaykh al-Makīn. It is very possible that the Beirut manuscript referred to does not differ from the work by Abba Sawirus we are discussing.[39]

Among the contemporaries of St Bulus, who wrote about this subject, it is worthwhile to mention here al-Rashid Abu al-

---

37 In Chapter Six on Christian Authors (or chapter 7 in some translations)
38 Refer Murqus Simaykah Pasha, **CATALOGUE VOLUME 1**, pp 45, no 91 (Theology 375). This book was mentioned with the abbreviated title **NOZOM AL-DORR WAL-GAWHAR** (Stringing together of Pearls and Jewels) in **HISTORY OF THE PATRIARCHS OF THE EGYPTIAN CHURCH** by Sawirus ibn al-Muqaffa, Vol II, p 11, translated and annotated by Aziz Suryal Atiya – Yassa Abd al-Massih – O.H.E. Khs. – Burmester (Le Caire, 1948), p 109.
39 G. Graf Geschichte d. Chr. Ar. literature, Bd. II p. 316

Khayr Ibn al-Tayyib who was a physician[40], priest and confidant of al-Amir Taqi al-Din Umar al-Muzaffar al-Qadi al-Fadl and vizier of Misr in the era of Sultan Uthman Salah al-Din. This scholar wrote the books TIRYAQ AL-UQUL FI ELM AL-USUL (Antidote of the minds in the Science of Fundamentals), KHULASAT MUTAQAD AL-MILLA L-MASIHIYYA WA-L-RADD ALA TA'IFATAY AL-ISLAM WA-L-YAHUDIYYA MIN MAWDU'ATIHIM WA-USUL MADHHABIHIM (Summary of the belief of the Christian religion and reply to the two communities of Islam and Judaism, from their writings and the fundamentals of their teaching) and RISALAT AL-BAYAN AL-AZHAR FI L-RADD ALA MAN YAQUL BI-L-QADA WA-AL-QADAR (A treatise of the most manifest elucidation in refutation of those who teach divine predestination and decree) in which he proves, using biblical and intellectual evidence, that man has free choice in defining himself.

We would also do well to mention that amongst the contemporaries of St Bulus was the scholar Mu'taman al-Dawlah Abu Ishaq Ibrahim Ibn al-Assal. He addressed this subject in depth and better clarified the true belief in three "chapters" in his well-known book entitled, MAJMU USUL AL-DIN WA-MASMU MAHSUL AL-YAQIN (Compendium of the principles of religion and the received tradition of what has been found to be certain)[41] Part Four: a) Chapter 56 "On Divine Predestination and decree, Fate, Mandates and Choice"[42]. b) Chapter 57 "On Wealth, Poverty, Health, Sickness and the Disparity Between People, etc"[43]. c) Chapter 58 "On the Belief in Life and Death in the Christian Church"[44]. His brother, al-Safi Abu al-Fadail

---

40   In the language of his time 'Met-tayeb'.
41   G. Graf, Catalogue pp. 49-50, ms. 125.
42   In the abovementioned manuscript from p 280 to p 298 – missing first page.
43   From p 298 to p 308 in the same manuscript.
44   From p 308 to p 310 in the same manuscript

ibn al-Assal, also refutes in his book called **KITAB AL-AWSAT** (Book of the Middle) what was in **KITAB AL-MAQALAT** (On the teachings) of its author the philosopher Abd-Allah al-Nashi, on erroneous belief regarding the question of predestination[45]. We also find, in the same era, Abba Mikhail Bishop of Atrib and Malig dedicating an article[46] to this subject by way of the question and answer to the effect: "Is life determined, meaning does man have a way of prolonging or shortening his life, or does the death of men happen by chance?"[47] Thus also al-Nushu Abu Shakir ibn Bu'rus al-Rahib explained two questions, amongst the fifty found in his work titled **KITAB AL-BURHAN** (The Book of evidence), one on choice and the other on predestination, and elaborated in their clarification[48]. If we mention this, it should not surprise the reader that St Bulus had been exposed to this question, especially if we realise that el-Sheikh Fakhr al-Dawlah had posed questions to the effect: "Are lifespans and livelihoods subject to predestination?". The manuscript no 341 in the Oriental Library in Beirut, mentions that the father the priest and monk Bulus, before being ordained a bishop over the see of Misr, had answered these questions[49].

St Bulus al-Bushi – A Capable Interpreter

St Bulus also excelled in the discipline of the interpretation of the Holy Bible. He left for us, a valuable commentary on the Book of Revelation. This book is known for its many complex mysteries and obscure dilemmas that are difficult to solve, and before the interpretation of which stood eminent Christian

---

45 Refer to G. Graf Geschichte, II Bd., p. 392.
46 The eighth article in a book containing 12 articles.
47 Refer to G. Graf Geschichte, II Bd., p. 416.
48 Refer to the aforementioned work, p. 431.
49 Refer to L. Cheiko, Catalogue, pp. 12-14; G. Graf Geschichte, II Bd. p. 360.

scholars, perplexed and disconcerted. So in interpreting some of its verses, they all considered various doctrines but could not find a way to a true and unified elucidation of its obscurities. It is worthwhile here to mention the scholars of the church of Alexandria, as in other churches, the sights of which never diverged from the interpretation of this great book that is called in its books the Book of the Apocalypse[50] or the Book of the Gillian[51]. In a manuscript collection known as the Pierpont Morgan Collection, a manuscript 28 (591) from page 11 to page 33 that contains a yet-unpublished compilation of commentaries on the Book of Revelation written in Sahidic and attributed to Abba Cyril the Great 24th patriarch of Alexandria.

The courage of St Bulus in composing a commentary on the Book of Revelation, proves that he was truly one of the most outstanding and eminent members of the church of Alexandria, as if the church at his time never lost its old reputation and renown for the interpretation of divine writings. His commentary was indeed comprehensive and complete. While the eminent ibn Katib Qaysar, one of the scholars of the Coptic church in the 13th century undertook a broader exegesis of that book, he did not complete it and so it is missing the last two chapters. It is apparent to a researcher, in the light of a comparison of the two commentaries, that the exposition written by ibn Katib Qaysar is not less valuable than that composed by St Bulus but rather surpasses it in length of explanation. Ibn Katib Qaysar knew of and had read St Bulus' commentary and upon reaching verse eighteen of the thirteenth chapter of Revelation in his own exposition, he had referred to it and had discussed it by saying, *"Bulus, bishop of Misr known as 'al-Bushi', mentioned in his commentary of this topic that there had been found in the Pharos of Alexandria five names that indicate this number (meaning the*

---

50 A word of Greek origin.
51 Syriac word meaning declaration or revelation.

the number of the beast, for it is the number of a man: His number is 666). The first four mentioned by Hippolytus, in particular the fourth, are conceptually very close to the word that is translated 'doubt'. As for the four names of which Bulus al-Bushi speaks, they do not in any way have this meaning. And though the number in it may agree, the meaning is not that of the beast rising up out of the sea or the one coming up out of the earth because these two beasts will come at the end of the ages as the Holy Gospel mentions. As from what I have seen of the conclusions drawn from the name of the designate sea beast, indeed this is not possible without inspiration. If there have been many inferences, how can we differentiate this name from others? The concealment of this name then is wisdom, lest a king or an instigator of a heresy take on the name and claim to be that beast."[52]

As for the Commentary on the Apocalypse by St Bulus al-Bushi, a complete and old handwritten manuscript may be found in the Coptic Museum in Old Cairo Number 52/2 (Rites 36)[53], comprised of 24 pages, 15 lines, measuring 20 by 14 in good handwriting, dated 1644 AD[54], penned by the deacon Yohanna ibn Ibrahim of the house of Yohanna Halbous known as ibn al-Moalemma (Refer to page 169 back). It may be observed that this copy contains the commentary without the text of the Apocalypse. We do not know who composed the commentary of the Apocalypse contained in the two manuscripts of the Coptic Museum in Old Cairo, one is Number 12 (Sacred 12), dated 1702 AD, and the other Number 708 (Theology 353), dated 16th century, and the text of two commentaries differ very

---

[52] Commentary on the Apocalypse of Saint John the Theologian by ibn Katib Qaysar, edited and footnoted by Father Armanius ibn Habashi el-Barmawi in Cairo 1655 AM, 1939 AD pp 223-224.

[53] Refer to G. Graf,op. Cit. P 21, ms 52-22, foll. 226v – 250v.

[54] The abovementioned author, p 21, 1684

little[55]. The last manuscript contains the commentary without the text of the Apocalypse. Until now, no one had cared to publish the handwritten manuscript of this commentary except when the reposed Father Armanius Habashy wished to publish **Ketab Sharh Sefr al-Ru'yā le ibn Katib Qaysar (Commentary on the Apocalypse), and found it was missing the last two chapters. He reportedly finished it by borrowing the commentary on these chapters by St Bulus so that the published commentary was complete. He utilised the manuscript found in the Coptic Orthodox Patriarchate Library in Cairo under the number 666**[56], from page 322 (back) to page 335 (back), dated 1400 – 1401 AD as opposed to the manuscript in the Coptic Museum No 52/2 previously described.

Since various Arabic interpretations of the Book of Revelation have emerged, the authors of some being unknown, and as there are also variations in the quotation of the Arabic text of the Revelation in some manuscripts, the scholar G. Graf has carried out a very thorough examination of each of the various Arabic translations of the Apocalypse, whether found in manuscripts or in published copies of the Holy Bible, to determine its source and whether it was translated from the Greek, the Syrian, the Bohairic or the Sahidic, as well as to ascertain the Arabic versions used by the interpreters of this book in their commentaries. He established that the majority of Arabic translations of the Book of Revelation were translated literally, with some departure, from the Bohairic text, and that the translators had inserted some readings from the Sahidic text.

He, however, refrained from giving his opinion on two manuscripts, one of which included in the interpretation of the Revelation by Father Bulus found in the Coptic Museum

---

55 G. Graf, Catalogue, p. 5, ms. 12; p. 262, ms. 708.
56 G. Graf, op. cit., p. 240, ms. 666; foll. 322 v-335v.

No 52/2[57], and the other a manuscript found in the Paris Public Library No 67 Arabic, dated to the 13th century by an unknown interpreter. Since the interpreter frequently refers to the commentaries of both Hippolytus pope of Rome, and St Bulus, the scribe wrongly attributes this commentary to them, as is apparent from the title at the beginning of this handwritten manuscript, which is, "The Book of the Apocalypse and its Interpretation, which is the Revelation Seen by John Son of Zebedee, One of the Twelve, the Evangelist and the Chaste, as interpreted by Saint Ankolitus (sic) Pope of Rome and Saint Bulus al-Bushi Bishop of Ahmuninn (sic)".[58] This scholar concluded his study by stating that these two manuscripts require further deep research before we are able to put forward a scholarly opinion about them relating to the source of the Arabic text of the Book of Revelation and its interpretation.

As an indication, I should mention that, to-date, research around the commentaries on the Revelation by St Bulus and his contemporaries have not yielded a scholarly conclusive and decisive result. At the Coptic Orthodox Patriarchate Library in Cairo, there is a manuscript that contains **"a part of the commentary on the Apocalypse by St Bulus al-Bushi" no 430/3(600) from page 65 (front) to page 95(back) dated from the 14th** or 15th centuries[59]. It is apparent, from comparing this commentary to that of the commentary on the actual book by the same author found in the Coptic Museum no 52/2[60], that the first is much longer than the second is. As I am unable to properly compare the two, I cannot ascertain whether the first is the work of St Bulus or that of another who

---

57   Ibid p21, ms 52/2
58   Copied verbatim. Refer to G. Graf. Arabische Ubersetzungen der Apokalypse (Biblica, t. X, 1929), pp. 193-194.
59   G.Graf, Catalogue, p. 157, ms. 430
60   G. Graf, Catalogue, p. 21, ms. 52-11

took it upon himself to expand upon St Bulus' commentary on the Apocalypse. The book AL-FIHRIS by Paul Sbath informs us that there is a manuscript that includes another commentary on the Apocalypse authored by "Deacon Ghobrial known as ibn al-khazen al-Kepty"[61] dated back to the 13th century, which is in the same century in which St Bulus lived.

Before I conclude my words on St Bulus as an interpreter of the Holy Bible, I would like to draw the attention of the reader to the book, KITAB AL-SHIFA FI KASHF MA-ISTATARA MIN LAHUT AL- MASIH WA-IKHTAFA (The Book of healing of what was hidden of the divinity of Christ) by the eminent author Abu Shakir ibn al-Rahib[62] Abu al-Karam Butrus ibn al-Muhadhab, deacon of the church of al-Muʿallaqah, in which among the various commentaries in AL-ASL AL-AWAL[63] "The First Trunk"[64] is the commentary on the Epistle of Saint Paul to the Hebrews Chapter 1 (1-4) by St Bulus. Some of his other commentaries are referred to in "The Third Trunk"[65] of the book. To-date we have been unable to find the complete commentary as we were unable to find the interpretation of some of the verses of this epistle in the compilation of the books of others. Based on this we may say that, if commentary on these verses of the Epistle of Paul to the Hebrews are not mentioned in the book ON THE INCARNATION mentioned previously, then it is possible to also attribute to St Bulus the book TAFSIR LE-RESALET BULUS ELA AHL AL-EBRANEIEN (A Commentary on Paul's Epistle to the

---

61 P. Sbath, al-Fihris (Supplément), Le Caire, 1940, p. (7). Ms. 2511
62 He wrote this book in 1268 AD a short time after the repose of Abba Bukus.
63 Containing the prophecies of the prophets
64 The book is structured on the basis of the image of the Tree of Life with a triple trunk.
65 Containing AL-AKWAL AL-RASOOLYA (The Apostolic Sayings). Not published by the publisher of KITAB AL-SHIFA Father Girgis. This book was published in Egypt and is not dated. The reader will find the commentary by St Bulus on pages 33-36.

Hebrews). As I was unable to view a copy of this book, I have deferred this subject to another time.

St Bulus al-Bushi – A Brilliant Dialectician

No religiously and academically educated Copt has, until now, devoted himself to the research of the debates and discussions that were exchanged between the Christians of Egypt and Muslims, in the middle centuries. In these, the Islamic side was given the name "al-Faqih" and who had to pose questions and objections, while the Christian side was given the name "al-Mugeeb" who had to explain and refute. Nor has any Copt being exposed to a study of the councils that were held, from time to time, between select Islamic elders and groups of Christian scholars, which were mostly convened by order of the Sultan or the king and held in his presence. None have published the replies that were issued now and then, in the form of 'letters' from Christian elders and their scribes as refutation and rebuttal of objections to the beliefs of the Christian religion and its literature, or as refutation of false claims levelled at Christian traditions or accusations directed at the clergy.

We cannot fail to mention that, in those days, some Muslim Imams would ask their Christian friends to explain to them the belief of the Christian faith such as the mysteries of the Trinity and the incarnation. They never hesitated in responding to this invitation and they explained the mysteries of the Christian faith and supported it with proofs refuting objections put forward by the people of Islam. It is sufficient for us here to mention that Al- Rashid Abu l-Khayr ibn al-Tayyib[66] had said in the preface of his book **KHULASAT (SUMMARY)**[67] that he had written it

---

[66] Lived in the first half of the 13th century. Refer to G. Graf, Geschichte, II,Bd., p.347

[67] Full name: KHULĀSAT MU'TAQAD AL-MILLA L-MASĪHIYYA

The life of St Bulus Al-Bushi

based upon a request from his Islamic and Jewish friends to clarify for them the mystery of the Holy Trinity and to prove that all prophecies were fulfilled in Christ. There is no doubt that this helpful research is quite ample and multifaceted, and would be demanding for whoever devotes himself to it, requiring familiarity with the spirit of that era and the circumstances of the religious atmosphere in it, as well as awareness of the details of its history. The researcher should also have experience with the meanings of religious expressions and terms which were commonly used by the Islamic and Christian scholars at that time.

If all these debates and discussions, that is the objections and their responses, were collected, accurately and faithfully copied from their original manuscripts, taking into consideration the time of their occurrence, and studied with the spirit of understanding, it would not be an exaggeration to say that this work would not be merely considered as a large volume to be left on a library shelf after only a cursory look. Rather it would be an important compilation and a great and indispensible reference for whomever wishes to deliberate upon the truth of the principled stances and religious vigour and enlightenment revealed by the intellectual class of the Coptic people in those ages.

Seventy years ago a German orientalist, the scholar Steinschneider, took this work upon himself[68] after collecting the manuscripts he was able to acquire at that time, studying it and preparing for it historical documents. Since the research

---

WA-L-RADD 'ALĀ' TA'IFATAY AL-ISLĀM WA-L-YAHŪDIYYA MIN MAWDŪ"ĀTIHIM WA-USŪL MADHHABIHIM (Summary of the belief of the Christian religion and reply to the two communities of Islam and Judaism, from their writings and the fundamentals of their teaching)

68 M. Steinschneider, Polemische und apologetische Literatur in arabischen Sprache (Leipzig, 1877)

of orientalists seventy years ago was not advanced but was in its early stages, and since the author had not read all manuscripts as most library and museum catalogues had not been established at the time, his research was incomplete and could not be fully accomplished due to the shortage of material. Fifty years after the emergence of this book, another orientalist named Fritsch[69], resumed research into this subject. He excelled, was beneficial and the results of his research indeed attained an extensive and successful stride forward, yet the critic can sense shortcomings with respect that which concerns debates between Muslims and Copts in Egypt and so with works compiled by Coptic scholars. This deficiency referred to was naturally due to the volume of divergent material contained in the various works and to these works not being published.

Research into this subject has shown that the elders of the Copts, particularly in the 13th century, in which lived St Bulus, and also in the 14th century, frequently devoted themselves to answer in their compositions the objections of the Muslim scholars and to defend their beliefs. But let not the reader suppose that among the Copts who wrote in the Arabic language, St Bulus was the first to descend into the arena of debate. No. Another scholar, Abba Sawirus ibn al-Muqaffa bishop of al-Ashmunayn, preceded him by approximately two hundred years. In the **HISTORY OF THE PATRIARCHS OF THE EGYPTIAN CHURCH** (Volume 2) it mentions that he had composed a book called **KITAB AL-MAJALIS**[70] (The Book of the Sessions) concerning retorts to the objections of some of the Muslim dialecticians. Then he said implicitly, *"... and I indeed confronted a man, one of their skilled speakers, with this objection*[71]*. Therefore, I challenged*

---

69 E. Fritsch, Islam und Chritentum im mittelalter (Breslau, 1930)

70 This work is lost.

71 Meaning the objection to "the corruption and modification" which, according to the allegations of their opponents, Christians have brought in to

the corruption of which he accused us and the other elders against what we have presented and he could not find a way."⁷²

He then wrote a book with the same objective which he called, KITAB AL-BAYAN AL-MUKHTASAR FI L-IMAN (A brief exposition of the faith). In it, he proved the complete accord between the understanding and the law (Christian) for the same objectors.⁷³ This was also true for the book KITAB ISTIBSAR AL-'AQL WA MISBAHO⁷⁴ (The understanding of the mind and its lamp). His friend Al-Wādih ibn Rajā wrote three books with the same intention. The first is called KITĀB AL-WĀDIH (The book of that which is clear/The confession), the second NAWĀDIR AL-MUFASSIRĪN WA-TAHRĪF AL-MUKHĀLIFĪN (The choice passages of the exegetes and the corruption of the opponents) and the third KITĀB AL-IBĀNA FĪ TANĀQUD AL-HADĪTH⁷⁵ (Clarification concerning the contradiction of the Hadith). In the late 12th century, Abba Mikhail, metropolitan of Damietta, directed a letter RISĀLA ILĀ AHAD OLAMA' AL-MUSLIMĪN⁷⁶ (Epistle to a Muslim scholar) to a Muslim scholar. Abba Butrus Sawirus al-Jamil, bishop of Malij during the late 12th early 13th centuries, then dedicated the three last treatises from a book he set down under the title KITĀB AL-BURHĀN (The book of the proof) to respond to questions posed by al-Faqih Gamal al-Din ibn Ahmad ibn al-Masry from Cairo⁷⁷. Here we mention

---

their faith.

72 Sevère ibn al-Moqaffa'; evêque d'Aschmounain, Histoire des Conciles "Second Livre" éd. Par L. Leroy (-P.O., t. VI, fasc. 4, Paris, 1911) p.40.

73 Not yet published.

74 P. Sbath, Al-Fihris (Catalogue de manuscripts arabes), 1re. Partie (Le Caire, 1938), p. 21, ms. 119

75 P. Sbath, Al-Fihris, 1re. Partie (Le Caire, 1938), p. 11, mss. 44, 45; p. 12, ms. 46 – G. Graf, Geschichte der christlichen arabischen Literatur, Bd. II, p. 319.

76 P. Sbath, Al-Fihris, 1re. Partie (Le Caire, 1938), p. 65, ms. 528

77 A manuscript of this book may be found in the Coptic Orthodox Patriarchate

a book entitled **HAL AL-SHEKOOK** (resolution of doubts) in which Father Butrus al-Sadamanti, a contemporary of St Bulus, responds to an issue raised by Imam Jamal al-Din Ahmad ibn Ahmad el-Masry about some meanings he requested him to summarise for him and to convince him of, (six chapters from the third treatise) [78].

It will suffice here for us to record what Copts wrote before the time of St Bulus, relating to answers to the questions and objections of Muslims. From this, it is apparent that, in this field, St Bulus followed in the footsteps of his predecessors. As for what his contemporaries, such as al- Rashid Abu l-Khayr ibn al-Tayyib, Al-Safi Abu l-Fada'il Majid ibn al-'Assal, Abba Mikha'il Usquf Atrib wa-Malij and those who came after them in the 14th century, compiled on this subject, it is hefty and requires an article to be dedicated to it. Abu l-Barakat Shams al-Ri'asa ibn Kabar informs us, in his catalogue of Christian writers that, before he became a patriarch, Abba Kyrillos Ebn Laqlaq wrote a polemic book. He says, "*The patriarch Abba Kyrillos Ebn Laqlaq had a dispute with a group of distinguished Muslims in the council of al-Malik al-Kamel ibn al-Malik al-Adil ibn Ayyub which was attended by the priest Bulus al-Bushi*"[79]. It happened that al-Malik al-Kamel ibn al-Malik al-Adil ibn Ayyub (1180 – 1238 AD) invited Kyrillos Ebn Laqlaq to a council of Muslim scholars. Abba Kyrillos chose St Bulus, who was a priest at the time, to accompany him so that he may assist

---

Library in Cairo. Refer to its description in G. Graf, Catalogue, p. 236-237, ms. 651a. III.

78 Refer to the **CATALOGUE OF THE COPTIC AND ARABIC MANUSCRIPTS IN THE COPTIC MUSEUM, THE PATRIARCHATE, THE PRINCIPAL CHURCHES IN CAIRO AND ALEXANDRIA, AND THE MONASTERIES OF EGYPT** Murqus Simaykah Pasha **PART 2 VOLUME 1**, p 268, no 596/6 and pp 113-114, (Cairo, 1932).

79 Refer to the **CATALOGUE** by Murqus Simaykah Pasha **PART 1**, p 45, no 91 (Theology 375) and p 210, (Chapter 7 in the classification of the Fathers etc.)

with his knowledge[80] in responding to the objections directed at him in the presence of al-Malik al-Kamel. It is said that the two displayed superior skill in answering all challenges so that el-Malik was very impressed with them and, following that, insisted on making Kyrillos Ebn Laqlaq patriarch in spite of the endeavours of the factions that opposed him.

This is what Abba Yusab of Fuwwa wrote in KITAB BATARIKAT AL-KORSI AL-ISKANDARI (The book of the patriarchs of the see of Alexandria) in the biography of Kyrillos Ebn Laqlaq: *"They convened for him a council along with the priest Bulus al-Bushi, in the presence of Abba Nicholas the Melkite patriarch, between the hands of al-Malik al-Kamil in the Citadel with the attendance of a large group of learned Muslim jurists. The Sultan praised his knowledge and thanked him for his explanation of the issues the Sultan had contrived and posed to him."*[81] Abba Kyrillos Ebn Laqlaq's choice of St Bulus to accompany him to this council is manifest evidence that, in the eyes of Kyrillos, St Bulus was a great scholar - a quick-thinker with a keen mind, well-versed in the tenets of religion, eloquent, skilled in oratory, capable of putting forward compelling arguments. Up until 1938, orientalists supposed that KITAB AL-MUJADALA (the book of disputation) was lost as they could not find it in any of the libraries, whether in Egypt or abroad. When, however, KITAB AL-FIHRIS (the catalogue) appeared in 1938, they became aware that a manuscript could be found with Father Constantine

---

80   As an aside, we mention that at the end of the 10th century, Abba Abraam Ebn-Zaraa the Syrian, 62nd Pope, called on the help of Abba Sawiris ibn al-Muqafaa, when he was called to a council before al-Malik El-Mu'izz, to debate with his vizier Yacoub ibn Yousef and the vizier's friend ibn Killis.

Refer to HISTORY OF THE PATRIARCHS OF THE EGYPTIAN CHRURCH, by Sawiris ibn al-Muqaffa', Vol. II, P. II, translated and annotated by Aziz Suryal Atiya-Yassa Abd al-Masih and O.H.E. Khs.-Burmester. Le Caire 1948, p. 92.

81   From a copy of the Syrian Monastery manuscript 8 History found in the Coptic Museum, p 144 (== p 213) dated from the end of the 17th century.

Khudari under the title, MUJADALA MA'A JAMA'A MIN AFADIL AL-MUSLIMIN BI-MAJLIS AL-MALIK AL-KAMIL IBN AL-MALIK AL-'ADIL IBN AYYUB, HADARAHU FIHA L-QISS BULUS AL-BUSHI (A disputation with a group of eminent Muslims in the majlis of al-Malik al-Kāmil ibn al-Malik al-'Ādil ibn Ayyūb, in which he was attended by the priest Būlus al-Būshī)[82]. Also, there does not exist a manuscript, containing either this debate or KITAB AL-MUJADALA, in the Vatican Library as Mr Guirguis Philotheos Awad as stated in his introduction to TAFSIR AL-RU'YA AL-QIDDIS YUHANNA AL-LAHUTI LI IBN KATIB QAYSAR (p. 6).

St Bulus al-Bushi – An Eloquent Ecclesiastical Orator

Not only did St Bulus offer the sons of his people excellent theological discourses of great value, that address dogma and questions in Christian literature, but we find that his zeal also pushed him to adorn his church with a precious necklace of sermons on the most important of the Lordly feats. Let not the reader entertain any doubt that the Coptic Church, before the time of St Bulus, was not devoid of such sermons. It would suffice for him to consult what is available in the libraries of old Coptic churches, the library of the Coptic Museum as well as museums all over the world that hold a number of manuscripts. Within these manuscripts may be found a large number of the sermons of Saints John Chrysostom, Gregory the Theologian and Basil of Cappadocia, translated from the Greek language to the Coptic and then to the Arabic, as well as the discourses of Saint Ephraim the Syrian, Abba Jacob of Serugh and Abba Severus of Antioch translated from the Syrian language to the Greek, then to the Coptic and finally to the Arabic. While we accept that these beautiful sermons are full of spiritual meanings

---

82 P. Sbath, al-Fihris, 1re. Partie (Le Caire, 1938), p. 62, ms. 504

and contain the spiritual nourishment and comprehensive guidance suited to the spiritual edification of the church, we must caution that they have lost much of their splendour, strength of expression and sweetness of words through their translation, and that their original style is not compatible with the current Arabic language of Egypt. In reality, the expressions written in them are, in many cases, difficult to discern and hard to understand for the Egyptian people even overlooking the inability to translate them, along with the inevitable incidence of distortion, errors and omissions in the copying of text by unskilled scribes or those who do not observe the principles of the art of transcription.

The HISTORY OF THE PATRIARCHS OF THE EGYPTIAN CHURCH says of Abba Sawirus ibn al-Mukaffa that, *"He had been a scribe and then he became bishop, and the Lord had bestowed upon him grace and power in the Arabic tongue, so that he wrote many books and sermons and controversies. He who read his books recognised his excellence and the soundness of his knowledge."*[83] Since none of these sermons have reached us, we cannot establish whether their subjects revolved around theological truths such as the mystery of the incarnation, or fasting, dying or the final judgement, or if they were written to explain the meanings and the standing of the Lordly feasts. It is very possible, that in the 13th century, the Coptic Church needed a comprehensive and harmonious collection of such sermons written in the classical Arabic language, provided that the ideas written in it, the expression and the style were completely compatible with the Egyptian mentality and its spirit. Therefore, it is right for us to award St Bulus the blue ribbon in this field, the field of oratory

---

83 HISTORY OF THE PATRIARCHS OF THE EGYPTIAN CHURCH By Sawirus Ibn Al-Mukaffa`, vol. II, p. II (Le Caire, 1948), p. 92

and eloquence at the lecterns of the churches in a perfect and refined Arabic language.

Shams al-Riyasah Abu al-Barakat ibn Kabar witnessed in the book **MISBAH AL-ZULMAH, FIIDAH AL-KHIDMAH** (Chapter Seven On the Righteous of the Nazarene (Copts) and their writings) of the quality of the sermons of St Bulus by saying, *"Bulus al-Bushi, bishop of Misr, has seven good sermons on the Lordly feasts"*[84]. This sermon collection is seven in number and includes sermons on The Annunciation, the Nativity of Christ, the Theophany, Palm Sunday, the Resurrection of Christ, the Ascension to heaven and Pentecost. Fortunately, most of the libraries of historical Coptic churches and monasteries retain this collection, which indicates that these sermons had the best standing in the souls of their hearers. However, in his catalogue of the compilations of Christian authors, Abu al-Barakat mentions that there are seven Lordly feast sermons by St Bulus, and we have discovered several manuscripts of another of his Lordly feast sermons, concerning the Suffering of Christ and His Crucifixion, to be read in the Sixth Hour of Great and Holy Friday[85]. As well as the manuscripts containing this sermon and mentioned by the scholar Graf[86], it may also be found in some of the manuscripts in the libraries of the historical churches of Old Cairo which date back to the 18th century.

I am unable to determine whether this sermon is included in *"the Lordly feast sermons by Bulus al-Bushi, bishop of Misr"* found in manuscript no. 236 (Theology 339) in the Coptic Orthodox

---

84 Refer Murqus Simaykah Pasha, **CATALOGUE VOLUME 1**, pp 45, no 91 (Theology 375) p. 210.

85 Mentioned in the manuscript of the Coptic Museum no. 77 (Rites 59) p. 132. Instead of "The Sixth Hour" is the following alert, "In the Times of the Hours".

86 G. Graf, Geschichte, II, Bd., pp.357-358.

Patriarchate Library in Cairo[87]. This manuscript was transcribed from a copy in the hand of Ibn Sadaqah, who states that he had copied it from a manuscript written by Abba Kyrillos (Ibn Laqlaq). If this sermon was found between the cited sermons in the mentioned manuscript, I do not understand why Abu al-Barakat ibn Kabar mentions only seven sermons of the feasts of the Lord by St Bulus. Regrettably only one of these sermons has been published; the sermon for the Feast of the Theophany[88]. That the reader may dwell upon the strength of these sermons, or even a small part of them, and may taste its spirituality, its excellent expression, its luminous interpretation glowing with the texts of the Holy Bible, these texts from which, in all his compositions, St Bulus never departed in the slightest. We will present here some excerpts from each of the eight sermons on the feasts of the Lord.

Excerpts from the Sermons of St Bulus Go Here

In these lines, we have attempted to collate what we have discovered, after much labour, in historical sources concerning the life and compositions of St Bulus al-Bushi. What is this writing but little nuggets and fragments so that, at the end of our journey, we ought to say that we have reached the attainment of our goals. Our intent, as far as the documents on hand have permitted, is to illustrate from it a true, though maybe weak, picture of this distinguished character. I say "the few sources on hand" while it should have never been so, had the reformative

---

87   Refer to the CATALOGUE OF THE COPTIC AND ARABIC MANUSCRIPTS IN THE COPTIC MUSEUM, THE PATRIARCHATE, THE PRINCIPAL CHURCHES IN CAIRO AND ALEXANDRIA, AND THE MONASTERIES OF EGYPT Murqus Simaykah Pasha and Yassa Abd al-Masih PART 2 VOLUME 1, p 98, no 236, (Cairo, 1942).

88   Refer to KITAB AL-TAAZI AL-ROHIA FI AL-MAYAMIR AL-SAYEDEAH (The Book of Spiritual Consolations in Lordly Feast Sermons) published at the expense of Murqus Guirguis, Egypt, 1642 AM p. 49-81

movement, in the arena of education and the publishing of books, begun by the well-remembered Abba Kyrillos IV, the Father of Reform, continued its course. It will not be so also, if the educated class of the Coptic people fulfils and encourages its mission, both financially and culturally, to publish the works of its scholars and if the Coptic Orthodox Patriarchate Library opens its doors to research.

May be an article such as this one, and its inherent shortcomings, will direct our attention to another shortcoming of equal importance, which is the lack of concern of those responsible in exploiting our repository of spiritual resources in the compositions of our fathers and scholars, and their failure to work in this field. Perhaps this is sufficient for us to understand and work so that our calls will reach those who care to move ahead. Let us join hand to hand and look seriously, at what is required of us by our position among Christian peoples, by our intergenerational heritage, by the labours of our mighty ancestors, and by the advancements of our era in scientific production and the study of historical artefacts. Let us say "Let us rebuild them though they are not demolished, tending to fall or in any need of restoration, but rather they are in need of raising if their foundations are established on earth."

From the little we have presented it is evident to the reader that St Bulus was indeed a man of religion in all the meanings of the word – a man of knowledge, a capable teacher bringing forth from his treasure old and new, a good shepherd. How could it be otherwise? While the Coptic people suffered a painful and violent disturbance, due to the perverted actions of a patriarch[89] who was a lover of money and a contravener of ecclesiastical laws. The disturbance worsened by the failure of the clergy in their duty towards the congregation and the

---

89   Abba Kyrillos Ebn Laqlaq as previously mentioned.

The life of St Bulus Al-Bushi

division of the leaders who were not guided by the good of the people. Throughout these obstacles, St Bulus declared the word of God in truth and integrity, carrying high, through his word and his pen, the lamp of the faith in the midst of his people. He reformed much of the imperfections, the distortions and the evils through the sobriety of his mind, and showed courtesy in the good governance of matters and the exertion of effort, as far as possible, in smothering the bitterness of the conflict that had broken out between the adversaries of Kyrillos and his friends before his ascension to the patriarchy. It is no secret that, as one of Abba Kyrillos' advisors and as his supervisor, due to his fondness for him as a colleague in many former works and as an old friend in the days of his monasticism in the monastery, he was a deterrent to his headstrong actions, a deflector of his ambitions, a soother of his raging emotions and a moderator of his resentment and cruelty toward his adversaries.

Thus, through his peaceful efforts, his great influence and his good example, he was able to preserve the church on many occasions from the evil of the actions of its religious leader. This patriarch lived the last three years of his life scorned by his people so that it was said he was hated and ostracised by the majority of the Coptic people, even by some of his faction who had turned against him, and so he withdrew to a monastery called the Wax (El-Shamaa) Monastery[90] (near Mit Shammas currently in Giza Governorate). He did not appear again before the congregation until he died on 10th March, 1243 AD at the same monastery, where he was also buried. It is not improbable for us to say that St Bulus was responsible, whether directly or indirectly, with

---

90 Also called the Monastery of the Devils (Dair al-Shayateen). Refer also to the description of this monastery and its history in Abu Salih, THE CHURCHES AND MONASTERIES OF EGYPT, ed. B.T.A. Evetts and A. J. Butler (Anecdota Oxon iensa, ser. Semit, t. VII, Oxford 1895) pp. 192-195 and also A BRIEF GUIDE TO THE COPTIC MUSEUM AND TO THE PRINCIPAL ANCIENT COPTIC CHURCHES OF CAIRO by Murqus Simaykah Pasha, Part II, Cairo 1932, p. 245.

counselling and advising his leader, after his turbulent life, to take refuge in a solitary life hoping that the quietness of the environment and the distance from worldly affairs and contact with his subordinates would facilitate his return to his senses in the twilight of his years, and so would conclude it penitent. Unfortunately, he was not up to the standard of his rare and exemplary gifts[91] since much mud had adhered to it.... We could not find in our sources the details of his affairs to help us know of the last days of St Bulus and of when he departed this life and found his Lord pleased and delighted in him, as one of the greatest minds and famous Copts who flourished in the first half of the 13th century, and became renowned for his piety and knowledge. For that reason, when subsequently a detailed history is written based on precise research and fair critique and in the light of manuscripts yet not studied, to enlighten the Coptic people, it will hold, for St Bulus al-Bushi Bishop of Misr, a bright page on which, with pride and admiration, will be recorded his exemplary life and his majestic deeds.

Father Yacoub Moazer

22 Tute 1666AM, the feast of the martyrdom of Julius of Aqfahs the Writer of the Biography of Martyrs.

---

[91] Abu Shaker Petrus, known as ibn Rahib, described him thus in the book HISTORY "He was a brilliant scholar possessing many talents except that he loved the amassing of money and the taking of simony. Consequently, people opposed him, insulted him and invoked councils for him in the presence of the representative of the Sultan and al-Adoul and the Vizier Mou-in al-Din (Hassan) ibn al-Sheikh" Petrus ibn Rahib CHRONICON ORIENTALE, ed. L. Cheikho S. I. (CSCO., Scriptores Arabici, textus, ser. 3a, t. I, Beryti, 1903) p. 142.

Section II
Selected Writings

The Eight Sermons on The Lordly Feasts

I

Feast of the Annunciation

Translated from the arabic edition
by Fr Mancarius Awad

In the name of the Father, the Son and the Holy Spirit, one God
Homily on the Life Giving Annunciation
By the honourable Saint Bulus al-Bushi
His prayers and blessings be with us to the last breath. Amen.

Glory to the divine power that reigns over all. The Word that created visible and invisible creatures. The sun of righteousness, who when He began to appear incarnate, illuminated the universe and removed from us the darkness of error. He drove away from us the beasts of destruction and the devouring wolves. He protected us from the dangers of perdition and showed us a path leading to eternal life. I ask of Your Grace, O true light that shone forth from the Father for salvation, I seek Your righteousness, O born of the Father before all ages, who secretly became incarnate, I implore Your mercies, O exalted above all authority and dominion, who humbled Himself for us. Enlighten my eyes and mind, O giver of light, who illuminates the depths of darkness so that I may speak of Your dignity. Give me a word, O Word of the Father, so that I may speak of the mystery of Your providence. Open my mouth, O giver of speech to the mute, so that I may proclaim Your glory. Give me from what is yours, O giver of abundance without indebtedness, and I will give You from what You have given me, for from You come good gifts and perfect talents.

Grant me knowledge so that I may give glory to Your noble incarnation. Grant me speech so that I may send praises for Your humility for the salvation of our kind. Inspire me with understanding so that I may offer prostrations and reverence for Your love that cannot be expressed. For You are the way, the truth, and the eternal life. And the door that leads to the fold of the spiritual flock.

I Feast of the Annunciation

Truly, the mystery of your providence, O God, surpasses all understanding and transcends all intellect. Just as You created creatures and brought them from non-existence into being, You have no need of them, but it is a favour from You.

When we transgressed the commandment, we were justly judged and fell from grace and eternal life. No creature was able to restore to us the life that has no end, because it was not suitable for it, and only the Lord created everything, and without Him, nothing was. As David said: By the word of God, the heavens and the earth were created. Then we knew that the Word who created creatures is the one who takes care of His creation and renews His creatures. He sent His word and healed them and saved them from corruption, so let us thank the Lord for His mercy and wonders among the children of men. Just as He brought them from non-existence into being. And when they lost eternal existence, it was by His justice that He transferred them from the non-existence of life to eternal existence in the kingdom without end, as befits Him.

He did not deliver this to us with His divinity because we are unable to bear it, but He condescended and incarnated, and brought us eternal life by uniting His eternal divinity with our humanity. Then He appeared defeating death and corruption through His holy resurrection, and brought us that life for that body taken from us. Just as the death we inherited from our father Adam was not strange to us but was inherited by us in relation to him, so also this life did not become strange to us but became ours in relation to the incarnation of the divine Word. Baptism and partaking in His living body by taking from His holy mysteries, as he testified saying: If you do not eat the flesh of the Son of Man and drink His blood, you have no eternal life, so the Creator made this covenant with His creation as no one can repair the work of His hands except Him.

Today, my beloved, the prophecy of the prophet Isaiah has been fulfilled, saying: Our salvation is not by an angel or a chief of angels, but by the Lord God of hosts. Also, David the Psalmist in our midst today sang saying: He bowed the heavens and came down, and darkness was under His feet. Then he informed us by declaring that His incarnation was hidden from the rulers and evil spirits. He said He descends like rain on wool and like dew when it falls on the ground. He means that He incarnates secretly and then completes the divine plan afterwards by declaration. And this is when He fills the whole universe with the glory of His divinity, because the Prophet did not remain silent but showed in His recitation the greatness of the Lord's work for salvation openly. He said: Justice and peace will abound in His days until the moon wanes. He meant by justice His equality among the Jews and all peoples at the beginning of the good news. And that He justified them freely by faith. He meant by peace that He broke down the wall that was a barrier in between and removed enmity and made reconciliation and peace between the heavenly and earthly. Like the word of the Apostle Paul. And He meant by the moon the ancient law, because it was named night as the Apostle also said: The night has passed and the day is near - because the moon is the light of the night.[1] ++++

As for Christ, He is the sun of righteousness as Malachi prophesied saying; "and the sun of righteousness is His name" - so when He appeared in the body, there was no longer any glory for the moon that was glorified in the night, as the Apostle testified saying: That which was glorified is now no longer glorified when compared to this excellent glory. And the Lord says: I am the light of the world, whoever follows me will not dwell in darkness but will live in the glory of the light of truth.

---

[1] With the coming of Christ, who is the Sun of Righteousness, the incompleteness of the Mosaic Law, which was referred to as the Moon, was revealed

I Feast of the Annunciation

Truly my beloved, the dignity of this feast is very great. Because it is the first of all feasts and the beginning of all joys, and the start of all delights. It is truly named the Feast of Annunciation. And it is not only for the Lady Virgin Mary, but for all of us believers. Because every annunciation to a people is typically specifically only for them, but this annunciation is for everyone.

Abraham was given the good news by the Lord of the birth of Isaac, but we did not receive from that any joy and promise of the birth of the Prophet Samuel. And also the mother of Samson the Mighty. Zechariah was given the news of the birth of John, but each of these had their own joy as the Psalms said: "The Lord looked on me to take away my reproach among people." But this annunciation today is for all the world, just as the Lord decreed to Eve saying, "In pain you shall bring forth children." This later became true for all her descendants. Like the decree that was upon Adam when it became applicable to all his descendants, so the angel said to the Virgin Lady, "Rejoice, full of grace, the Lord is with you." That joy and grace became for all of us believers. Because the Lord has come to us on earth in a wondrous body. And we have seen His glory, the glory as of the Only-Begotten Son, full of grace and truth.

And just as the angel, when he announced to the shepherds the birth of the Lord, said to them, "Behold, I bring you good tidings of great joy which will be to all people, for there is born to you this day a Saviour, who is Christ the Lord." So is the joy of this noble feast today. It is a general announcement for all the world, because it announces to us the coming of the Lord to us, and the union of His incomprehensible divinity with our nature, the weak nature that was perishing, making it strong, victorious over death, and conqueror of Satan and his hosts.

Today, my beloved, we must rejoice - because in it we see the Lord shining from on high to give light to those sitting in darkness and the shadow of death. Today we celebrate the mystery of the Lord to seek His people for salvation, and His creation is promised healing and righteousness. And because when the illness intensified and the ailment increased and the cure became difficult, there was a need for treatment from the skilled Physician who is able to do all things, the healer of souls and bodies. He is the incarnation of the divine Word.

He is the eternal Word of mercy. The complete embodiment of perfection, the unstoppable power. The gift that does not change. The likeness that is impossible. The example that does not fade. The type that is not altered. The property that nothing can match. The holy one that remains pure. The eternal image that does not corrupt. The commander that contains the glory that never fades. The sun of righteousness that never sets. Light from light, true God from true God. Begotten, not created. Equal to the Father in essence, although the Father is called God, and the Son is called God because of the one divine essence. And likewise the Holy Spirit. But it is not said that there are three gods, for these are the special characteristics of the divine nature, three persons in one divinity.

Gregory the Theologian said: When you say God, you are speaking of the Father, the Son, and the Holy Spirit. Because the divine nature does not attribute anything beyond this, nor does it include anything less. And yet we do not worship three, lest we resemble the nations who believe in many gods. Nor do we become like the Jews who deny the word of God and His Spirit, for both understanding are equal even though their expressions differ.[2]

And so we believe that the Word was born of the Father in an eternal birth that was necessary, and He willed to be incarnate

---

2 The author means that the error is the same among the nations who believe in the multiplicity of gods and among the Jews who deny the Holy Trinity.

I Feast of the Annunciation

from the holy Virgin Mary of the house of David, of the tribe of Judah, of the seed of Abraham, so that the world could see Him, and to save the likeness with His likeness³. He sent a holy archangel before Him to announce that the incarnate one is the Lord, for where the heavenly Lord and King is, there are His celestial servants.

Come into our midst today, O holy evangelist Luke the physician, preacher of life. For you have informed us of the plan of the incarnation from the very beginning. When it was the sixth month, meaning of Elizabeth's pregnancy, Gabriel the angel was sent from God.

Oh, the honour bestowed upon this angel above all the spiritual beings, for he was entrusted with the secret of the plan, and he went before the Lord in this annunciation of truth, for the interpretation of the name Gabriel in Hebrew is man of God, and it is a secret of the incarnation, that God united with man through the mystery of incarnation⁴.

He declared it in a city of Galilee called Nazareth. This was to fulfil what was said in the prophets, that He would be called a Nazarene. He said: To a virgin betrothed to a man named Joseph of the house of David. It was mentioned that she was betrothed to Joseph so that the Lord's plan of the incarnation would not be hidden from the devil. For the prophecy mentions that the virgin will conceive and bear a son, and His name shall be Immanuel. And that is why the announcement was made after the Lady Virgin left the temple to the house of Joseph to conceal the mystery of her pregnancy.

---

3   That the hypostasis of the Son took upon Himself the form of man through His incarnation in order to save man through His suffering while He was carrying the form of man.

4   That is, the meaning of the word Gabriel (man of God, which contains a clear reference to incarnation because his name combines divinity and humanity).

And his saying that He is from the house of David to declare that the tribe of David was preserved and did not mix with other tribes for the sake of incarnation. Then after that, they mixed after the ascension of the Lord for about forty years in the rule of Emperor Vespasian when he destroyed the holy temple, killed the Jews, and scattered those that were left on the face of the earth. He said the name of the Virgin Mary to confirm the new to her. She is from the house of David as will be explained. He said, and when the angel entered upon her, he said to her: "Rejoice, O full of grace, the Lord is with you." The angel gave her peace from God filled with joy to remove Eve's sorrow. Just as when she ate from the tree of disobedience to obey Satan, the king who ruled over her, and took possession of her kind, so too when she obeyed the message saying, let it be as you say, God the Word dwelt in her and filled her with every grace and joy, and this extended to our kind, bestowing salvation upon us freely and walking with us on earth.

When she heard this, she was troubled by his words and thought, saying, what is this peace, meaning that she had not spoken to anyone because she was raised in the temple in seclusion and tranquillity, worshiping God day and night. The Gospel revealed her virtue. And when she was troubled by the voice of the angel, she did not let go of the reserve she had accustomed to and the tranquillity in which she had been raised. She did not scream or push back his words altogether, she thought to herself alone, saying, what is this strange peace today, so the angel addressed her with calmness suitable for her, saying, "do not be afraid, Mary". For this is the usual appearance of the sight from God and His pure angels, when it appears it removes fear and gives peace and tranquillity. As for the appearance from Satan, it increases fear upon fear and anxiety upon anxiety. And thus the saints recognized the appearances from the devil and his soldiers. When the angel calmed her fear, he began to give her good news, saying: "Because you have found favour from God", meaning that he chose her for the noble incarnation above all humans to be a dwelling place for God the Word, and from her our salvation is realised, so what grace could be more honourable and what gift could be better than this honour?!

Blessed are you, O new heaven on earth, O Mary. For you have deserved to be called the mother of God, the mother of Christ the Lord, the bearer of the Word, and His servant. The one with powerful intercessions.

He said: "And you will accept this pregnancy and give birth to a son", meaning that he is incarnated in reality from her without resemblance or imagination with humanity in its entirety. He resembles us in everything except sin. And thus she gives birth to Him and completes the mystery of His plan. And he said: And his name will be Jesus, interpretation of Jesus the Saviour. And thus he was named as per His work, as per His saying: The Son of Man came only to save and redeem those who were lost.

Then the angel began to inform her by declaring, saying: "He will be great and will be called the Son of the Most High", meaning that even though He is born in the flesh, He is still the Son of the Most High because he is the incarnate God in a mystery ineffable, born of Him eternally. A Being without beginning and will be without end. And by His name He will be called, meaning by the incarnation the mystery of the Son of God has been revealed. Then the angel began to show the perfection of the incarnation, and that the Virgin is the daughter of David, saying: "And the Lord God will give him the throne of his father David." He confirmed that the Virgin is unlike any other, and how could that be, if not for the incarnation of God the Word who willed to be incarnate from the Virgin without the seed of man. As Solomon said, "Wisdom has built her house."

And the holy Mary, due to her great faith in God and her good conviction, despite this strange news that was previously unheard of, believed the good news and believed that it would be for her!! And the Almighty God supported her with His Spirit that came upon her. So she directed her desires towards the Lord.

And she longed for the word that the angel had informed her of, and she desired it to be for her, and she answered him saying: "Behold the maidservant of the Lord, let it be to me according to your word." And only after she said this, the Sun of righteousness shone upon her, because He did not want to force Himself upon the human nature that He had given the choice of will and the power of freedom since the beginning, until she first desired it by the will of God from the Spirit[5]. After she said this the angel departed from her. Meaning that when he completed the message and the Lord came in the amazing incarnation, He allowed him to depart in peace, because he had completed what was required of him in the service he was sent for.

Today, my beloved, the saying of David is fulfilled, who said: "Listen, O daughter, consider and incline your ear; forget your people and your father's house. And the king will desire your beauty. For he is your lord; worship him." Indeed, she heard and forgot everything in this world when she attained the supreme elevation and honour. But what is the beauty that the eternal God desired? Is it worldly splendour? That is not the case. For the prophet also informed us of this beauty in the psalm, saying: "All glorious is the princess in her chamber, with robes interwoven with gold." By this, he meant the soul that speaks with purity of virtues. And Peter the apostle writes and

---

5 That is, the incarnation took place at the moment when the Virgin surrendered her command to God and agreed with longing and joy to the presence of the Son, the Word, in her womb, and that the incarnation did not take place by force in the pure Mary, but rather by her desire and freedom.

confirms this speaking beauty, saying: "Your beauty should not come from outward adornment, such as elaborate hairstyles and the wearing of gold jewellery or fine clothes. Rather, it should be that of your inner self, the unfading beauty of a gentle and quiet spirit, which is of great worth in God's sight."

This is the beauty of the Virgin Mary, who adorned herself with virtues, her inner beauty. As for her outward appearance, she did not care about anything in the world, little or much. Her concern was to draw closer to her Lord and to be pure in body and soul, as the prophet teaches us.

And thus, the blessed Mary deserved to be called the second tabernacle, in which the glory of God dwelt. For the first tabernacle, made by Moses, was constructed with fine linen and blue, purple and scarlet yarn, and skilfully worked by a craftsman. In it were the altar vessels of gold and silver, with the lampstand and the Ark of the Covenant which was overlaid with pure gold. Inside the tabernacle was adorned with beauty. As for the outside, it was covered with goat hair, making it appear humble. But inside, it was majestic in value, honour, and beauty. The sight was delightful, and the glory of the Lord was in it. And so, the blessed Mary, her appearance was humble, modest, and pious. But her inner self was very glorious, shining with her soul attached to God, who looks upon her, as written in the book of Samuel the prophet: "For the Lord sees not as man sees: man looks on the outward appearance, but the Lord looks on the heart."

You are the bush from which God spoke to Moses with a burning fire that did not consume its branches, and its leaves did not change colour. If anyone doubts the work of the Lord through him, let his mind be directed to that lowly bush with thorns and no fruit. Why didn't God speak to Moses from a tree with fruits? This is further emphasized by saying: "I am the God of Abraham, the God of Isaac, and the God of Jacob." Then he commanded him to go down to Egypt, and the proof of that and its validity was only confirmed when he descended to Egypt and performed miracles by the command of God and led the people out with a strong hand, making it clear that the one who spoke to Moses in the bush was the Lord God of hosts.

You are the mountain that Daniel testified about, from which a stone was cut without human hands, which is the precious stone, the Lord. Who incarnated from you without seed of man, and became a great mountain and filled the inhabited world. This is the glory of His divine nature over all creation. Even if time and logic fall short for me to praise your glory as you deserve, O pure Virgin in every way, how can I offer honour and worship to the Lord God who incarnated from You. I ask for the goodness of His righteousness and the abundance of His mercy, which, out of His love, humbled Himself for our salvation, and honoured our lowly nature by uniting with it, to look upon us with the eye of compassion from the heavens of His holiness. And to forgive our sins, overlook our faults, pardon our sins, and help us to work with joy.

And if we have no advocate before Him, we ask of Him through your intercessions, O pride of our race, O Virgin with strong intercessions. Because you have received from Him grace, and became to Him a better advocate than the heavenly angels and all creation, those who were and those who will be also. For from you alone is the mystery of the incarnation.

Great is the glory of this feast, my beloved, because it is the first of the seven divine feasts. Just as on Sunday - the first of the seven days - God created all creation as a whole. Then He distributed it in the other days, as witnessed by the Book of Creation, saying: "In the beginning God created the heavens and the earth, and the earth was formless and void. And darkness was over the face of the deep. And the Spirit of God was hovering over the face of the waters. And God said, 'Let there be light,' and there was light. And God saw that the light was good. And God separated the light from the darkness, and called the light Day and the darkness Night. And there was evening and there was morning on the first day. So God created the angels from that light, as well as the lights and the stars. Then he gathered the water on the earth and it became seas. And the dry land appeared. Then he created plants and trees from the earth and raised them and made them grow."

And He created the fish and the birds from the water. Then from the earth He also created the animals and made among them humans. And He honoured them with the great speaking spirit. It is true that all were created on Sunday and distributed in the other days, and likewise this noble feast. I mean the feast of the Annunciation, in which the whole plan that God intended to complete with the marvellous incarnation was complete in the other six divine feasts with the rest of the plan's mystery. Without the incarnation He is invisible in His divinity and not suffering. He chose the mystery of the incarnation so that creation may see Him. He completes His plan with the body. He suffers for us and rises. He gives us victory and rises from the dead. He took on our human flesh to give us the gift of His Holy Spirit in the second birth, which He poured out on His pure apostles, after the completion of the fifty days. He descended to us, who is above all, to raise the body, which was below to the heights of the heavens and raise it above the rulers, kings, and powers. And above every name that is named. And to reconcile between the heavenly and earthly beings, He completed all of this through the incarnation. However, we see people who do not care about this feast as much as the rest of the divine feasts, because it falls during the holy forty-day fast. They think that the honour of the feasts lies in food, drink, and worldly pleasures. But it is not so, because the Lord says, "Take heed to yourselves, lest your hearts be weighed down with carousing, drunkenness, and the cares of this life, and that Day come on you unexpectedly like a snare." For it has been confirmed that excessive indulgence in these things hardens the heart and drives away humility. And the soul has another food besides this, spiritual food, that remains and does not disappear. For the Lord also teaches us, saying: "Do not labour for the food which perishes, but for the food which endures to everlasting life, which the Son of Man will give you, because the reading of the Scriptures, which is by the Spirit, is your honour. The chanting of the word of God is your pride. Standing in prayer is your comfort. Persevering in supplication to God is your hope. Your connection with Him with diligence to remember His holy name is your nourishment. As David says, "My soul shall be satisfied as with marrow and fatness when I remember You."

Your approach to Him through virtuous deeds is your drink. As it is said, "Let him who thirsts come. And let him who desires take the water of life freely." Preserve your bodies with purity and chastity, not the splendour of your clothing. Control your senses from sinful matters, for the brightness of your souls. Extend your hands in mercy and He will forgive your sins, as it is said, "Be merciful, just as your Father also is merciful." Remove hatred from your hearts towards your brothers, your guide at the time of your prayers, and you will find yourselves saying, "Forgive us as we forgive those who wrong us." Change bad habits with good ones, to your honour. Strive to abolish vice and strive to establish virtue, having a crown of glory placed on your heads.

This is the feast of the generation that seeks the Lord. They seek the face of the God of Jacob, not with the feasts and drinks that spoil and become worthless, for if they increase, they have inherited matters that lead to error, as Paul the Apostle admonishes us, saying: "If you live according to the flesh, you will die. But if you put to death the deeds of the body by the Spirit, you will live forever." He also said, "Do not get drunk on wine, which leads to debauchery. Instead, be filled with psalms, hymns, and spiritual songs." Let us now celebrate the divine feasts as is fitting, so that we may rejoice with all the saints in the heavenly kingdom, the place of rest for the saints where sorrow and gloom are far removed.

We ask the Lord, who has the power to guard our people and help us achieve the salvation of our souls, to rest the souls of our dead, to protect us from trials for the remainder of our lives, and to qualify us all for a share with the saints in the eternal kingdom and everlasting life through the intercession of our pure Virgin Saint Mary, through whom the Word of God was incarnated, and through the intercession of the pure apostles, all the martyrs, and the righteous saints. May those who please the Lord with their good deeds be pleased by Him now and forever Amen.

II

Glorious Nativity

Translated from the arabic edition
by Fr Mancarius Awad

In the name of the Father, the Son and the Holy Spirit, the one God, to whom be glory forever. Amen

Homily on The Glorious Nativity

By the honourable Abba Bulus al-Bushi

His prayers and blessings be with us to the last breath. Amen.

Glory to you, O born of the Father before all ages, who was born today in the flesh from the Virgin for our salvation. Glory be to You, O Sun of righteousness, who shone upon us today with the rays of His divinity and illuminated the universe. Glory be to you, O Christ the King, the owner of heaven and earth, who took the form of a servant to give His servants the freedom that befits them. Glory be to you, O heavenly Creator, who raised His earthly creation and united them with the heavenly ones. Glory be to the one who illuminated with rays of His divinity, through the virgin birth, the farthest corners of the earth until they came to Him prostrating. Glory be to the one whom they searched for in the law and the prophets for His birth and came to Him worshipping[1]. Glory be to the one whose birth the heavenly beings glorify and the earthly beings worship.

I ask for your righteousness, O You the One who lifted the shame and disgrace from us by His birth from the Virgin. I seek your love, O One who humbled Himself and became with us on earth, while He remained in heaven!! I cry out to You, O One who became human and did not forsake the honour of His divinity that belonged to Him before all ages. Shine the ray of Your divinity in the depths of my soul, O Sun of righteousness, do not be silent, O marvellous Son. Guide me, O light of truth, who guided the Magi to know Him, so that I may proclaim

---

1 He is referring to the Magi

II Glorious Nativity

Your humility and coming to us. Grant me the gift of speech, O One who freely gave salvation to the world. And in His humility, He became with them on earth as a human while His divinity was present everywhere. So that I may open my mouth and proclaim Your coming in every proclamation of You.

O Christ, who was born today from the Virgin in the flesh. I praise You with the angels and hasten to You with the shepherds. To You I bow down with the Magi. For Your noble coming I search[2] with the scribes of the law. I sing with the prophets and present their testimonies. I proclaim You with the evangelists and present their writings. I open my mouth with Your Holy Name. And with Your glorious memory, my lips shall rejoice. I cry out with a voice more melodious than the horn. And I rejoice and exult in this glorious feast.

Today I remember what the prophets spoke and what the messengers proclaimed. Come into our midst today, O Jacob, Israel, the father of the tribes and the chief of the clans. Inform us of the dignity of the coming of the true Christ to us. "The leader of the Jews will not disappear from Judah, nor the lawgiver from between his feet until the one who has the authority over all comes, and upon him the nations rely, and in him the nations hope." Indeed, the prophecy is very clear and does not need another prophecy with it. This is because the king was from the tribe of Judah in the children of Israel until the coming of the Christ. So when the birth of the Christ the Lord happened, the nations ruled over them. And they wrote their names in the census. As the evangelist Luke testified saying, "In those days", meaning the birth of the Lord in the flesh, he said: "A decree went out from Augustus Caesar that all the world should be registered", and it was made known to us that the time that had

---

2 Because the writers of the law were busy examining the prophecies about Jesus Christ

passed was not registered yet. And he said: "This census first took place while Quirinius was governing Syria." Meaning that this was the first census for the Jews to be taxed. For the decree from Caesar, the king of Rome, was to show us that the Romans had authority over them. And the one appointed before him, Quirinius, was responsible for writing the names and collecting the census, because Herod the Great, the father of Archelaus, was at that time in charge of the tax.

And thus it was completed that at the birth of the Christ, the kingship and rulership were taken away from them, and they became under the rule of the kings of the nations!! Because God knew the hardness of their hearts. Thus the coming of the prophets ended because the Law and the prophets were until John as the Lord said. And from him He proclaims the kingdom of God, which is the coming of the glorious Lord to us. Even to this day, the Jews cannot surpass these well-known prophets who were before the incarnation of the Christ. They are twenty-four prophets and this sign confirms that the Christ has come. Because he took away from them the kingship and rulership and nullified the coming of the prophets. He also took from their hands the temple in which they served according to the ancient Law. The one who offered sacrifices of animals and the blood of goats and the purification of the lepers, he completed that with his body and blood and the purification of baptism. Those who obeyed Him believed in Him. And those who did not obey Him scattered in the corners of the earth under the rule of the kings of the nations.

Today, my beloved, the prophecies of the prophets have been fulfilled in the birth of the Lord from the Virgin Mary.

Isaiah announces this saying: "Behold, the virgin shall conceive and bear a son, and shall call his name Immanuel, which means God is with us."

II Glorious Nativity

Ezekiel the prophet teaches us a strange secret, saying: "I saw in the east a closed and sealed gate with a wonderful seal that no one entered except the Lord of hosts. He entered and exited without opening the gate or changing the seal." This is the secret of his prophecy regarding the immaculate birth of Mary without human seed. He informs us that the one born from her is the Lord of hosts. That is why He preserved her immaculateness in His incarnation and in His birth from her, and even after His birth, because He has power over all things.

Isaiah says, "For unto us a child is born, unto us a Son is given, and the government shall be upon His shoulder, and His name shall be called Wonderful Counselor, Mighty God, Everlasting Father, Prince of Peace." The prophet confirmed His birth in the flesh for us. Then He showed us that He is the Mighty God, the Everlasting Father.

Jeremiah informs us that God will be with the people on earth, in a miraculous incarnation, saying: "God will come down to earth and walk among the people."

And Ezekiel teaches us the same, saying: "They will know that I am the Lord their God when I appear among the people and speak to them openly."

Similarly, David prophesied saying: "God appears in Zion", meaning that those who are called gods are only so because the word of God came to them. "As for the one who appears in Zion, he is the God of gods in truth and the Lord of lords. All flesh shall worship him as divine, not by a borrowed name." Isaiah the prophet said the same: "The word of God shall appear in Jerusalem, and the law shall come forth from Zion."

David teaches us that the one born from the Father before all ages is the one born from the Virgin in the flesh, saying, "The Lord said to me, 'You are my son, today I have begotten you'

– meaning the birth in the flesh – and he said, "I have begotten you from the womb before the morning star," also "God shall come openly, and our God shall not be silent," and "The Lord has sent you a rod of strength from Zion, rule in the midst of your enemies," and "Zion shall say, a man was born in her, and the Most High established her."

Isaiah the prophet said, "The Lord will come truly, and will appear on the earth."

Nahum the prophet said, "Behold, I am coming and will dwell in you," says the Lord, the commander of all.

Zephaniah the prophet said, "Sing aloud, O Zion; shout, O Israel! Rejoice and exult with all your heart, O daughter of Jerusalem! The Lord has taken away the judgments against you; He has cleared away your enemies. The King of Israel, the Lord, is in your midst; you shall never again fear evil."

Zechariah the prophet said, "O daughter of Zion, behold, I am coming and I will dwell in your midst, declares the Lord."

Malachi the prophet said, "Behold, the Lord is coming, and the Sun of righteousness shall rise with healing in its wings."

Truly, my beloved, the Sun of righteousness has risen for us today with the birth from the Virgin. The one born of the Father before all ages, an eternal birth without beginning, not comprehended or confined by time. He was born today for the salvation that minds cannot grasp or comprehend, manifesting Himself today in the flesh. He who is feared by the intellectual powers. He surpasses all authority and dominion, and His divine honour exceeds all creatures. He chose to humble Himself and go against our poor nature, sitting on a throne of glory. Above the highest heavens, He appeared among humans and did not forsake the height of His honour. Instead, He fills all with the simplicity of His divine nature that cannot be contained.

II Glorious Nativity

Very great is the dignity of this glorious feast. Today, my beloved, we must all honour and glorify it, rejoice and be happy. Consider the rulers of this world and the kings of the earth, who die and their reigns pass away, yet they honour the memory of their birth and commemorate it among themselves with their nobles every year, as it is written, "When Herod's birthday came, the daughter of Herodias danced before them and pleased Herod, so he promised with an oath to give her whatever she might ask." Therefore, it is fitting for us to rejoice and celebrate with great joy on the day of the birth of the King of kings, the Lord of lords, the One who reigns with His power over all creation. Especially since His incarnation and birth were not for His own sake, but for us and our salvation. He descended from heaven, was incarnate of the Virgin Mary, and was born in the flesh so that we may be born spiritually. He humbled Himself to exalt us, united with our lowly nature to give us the gift of the Holy Spirit. And this noble assembly today is not devoid of its nobles[3] and eternal rulers! They are present with us, speaking to us, and among us, speaking words given to them by the Spirit. Who are they? They are His holy prophets, His noble apostles, and His righteous nobles, who are enlightened with His mystery, bestowed with the gift of His Holy Spirit. As for the prophets, their call has preceded, those who prophesied about the Spirit coming in His glory. And so began the call of the apostles, the loyal lords, rulers, and leaders of all nations. Rivers of living water, as prophesied by the prophet Ezekiel, saying: "The beautiful in their warnings." And as the prophet Nahum prophesied, saying: "How beautiful are the feet of those who bring good news, whose voices have gone out into all the earth and their words to the ends of the world."

---

3 He means that the prophets who predicted the coming of the Saviour were present at the celebration of His glorious feast.

Come now, O evangelists, bearers of life, so that we may receive from you the sword of the word. For you are witnesses of the Word of God, His service, and His nobles, and through you, minds are enlightened.

When Matthew the evangelist says Jesus was born in Bethlehem of Judea, he wanted to mention Bethlehem specifically to remind us that the prophets mentioned Christ would be born in Bethlehem, because he wrote his gospel in Hebrew. He also mentioned the genealogy, starting from Abraham, because the genealogy ends specifically in the reproduction of the Hebrews only.

As for Luke, when he wrote his gospel in Greek, he did not want the Gentiles who believed in Christ to be saddened that Christ was not from them according to the flesh, so he started from below and worked his way up until he reached Abraham. He did not stop there, but extended the genealogy to Noah because he came as a father of all tribes and tongues. Then he added to this the philosophy of confirming the spirit and ended with Adam, to explain to them the genealogy of the Torah in summary. It delights us all believers that Christ incarnated from the lineage of our father Adam and was called the second Adam, to be a father and leader of all the living, as befits His divinity and as the provider of all blessings and the first to rise from the dead.

And when Matthew wrote His gospel in Hebrew in Jerusalem, He explained matters to the Jews who believed in the Law. Then He mentioned in the genealogy two women from the nations, Thamar and Rahab, to show them that they shared in reproduction with the nations and that their lineage is from them, so they should not refuse to share in faith with them and mingle with them, especially since baptism has purified everyone. Then he began to speak little by little, and took testimony from the prophets, saying, "When Jesus Christ was born in Bethlehem

II Glorious Nativity

of Judea in the days of King Herod", he mentioned Herod to recount what happened to him with the Magi and his search for the newborn and the killing of the children.

He said, "When the Magi came from the east to Jerusalem saying, 'Where is the newborn King of the Jews? For we have seen his star in the east and have come to worship him.'"

Oh, what a wonderful secret, and divine plan, and how God arranged things gently, and attracted these Magi to Him from outside beliefs they were holding onto. For He attracted these Magi to Him from their craft in which they were raised, and they were delighted with it, because they were from the land of Persia, from the lineage of Balaam the soothsayer. They had teachings from him, and they could predict the movement of the planets, except that when they read and understood about the true King Christ, their hearts did not incline towards the worship of idols. When God knew the truth of their conviction, and that they submitted to the truth, He showed them a heavenly power resembling a star!! And nothing like it had ever appeared among all the planets, which indicates that the one born at that time would rule over all kingdoms and presidencies. His reign would never end. The evidence that it was a power from God and not among the visible planets, is that His actions were different from all the other stars.

Firstly, He appeared to them during the day and disappeared at night, which indicates that the newborn is the day and the Sun of righteousness. Then He moved left[4] to right, slightly deviating to the west, going from Persia to Jerusalem. This indicates that His perfection would be in Jerusalem. He walked as they walked, and stood as they stood. This indicates that the Lord is compassionate towards humanity, and completes

---

4 The saint uses a play on words for the word شمال (shemal) which can mean either 'north' or 'left'

physical things. His walk was wonderful, humble, and close to them. This indicates the humility of the Lord born in the flesh, being with us on earth while exalted above all with His divinity. His closeness to them was to lead them, like a guide, to the destination they sought, straight without deviation, to show that the newborn is the one who leads us in all goodness and guides us to the heavenly Jerusalem - the kingdom of heaven - as He said, "I am the way, the truth, and the life." Despite all this, the light of the sun could not hide Him, indicating that the newborn surpasses all beauty and excellence, and excels above all names, whether seen or unseen. As David prophesied about Him, saying: "He is fairer than the sons of men." Meaning, even though He appeared in the flesh and was found in the form of a man, He surpasses all in the beauty of His divinity.

When the star led them to Jerusalem, it disappeared from them by design. So that they may announce the birth of the Lord Christ to those who were waiting for Him - I mean the Israelites in the flesh - to show that the nations surpass them in faith and are favoured over them. And the Magi, due to their great effort and love to see the newborn Christ, when the star disappeared from them, they did not wait, but asked like messengers of good news, saying, "Where is the newborn King of the Jews?" And this is because they fulfilled His command well. And that is why they endured the long journey and great hardship. And why is that? They said, "Because we saw His star in the East." And they did not say, "We came to see Him," but they said, "We came to worship Him." I mean that the star appeared to them first from the eastern sky and approached them because they were in the land of Persia, as mentioned earlier, towards the north, turning towards the east. It indicates that the newborn from heaven shone upon us. And we returned from the left to the right. Then they acknowledged that they approached Him prostrating, to indicate their certainty of knowing him.

II Glorious Nativity

The Holy Scriptures say, "When Herod heard this, he was troubled", and because of his lack of understanding, he thought that He was an earthly king, who would take away his kingdom and destroy him and his kindred altogether, and he did not understand that He was the eternal King, the Lord from heaven, who said, "I have not come to destroy the souls of men, but to give them life." And He also said, "I give my life for my sheep." And likewise, Jerusalem was troubled altogether when they heard that the awaited Christ had been born, and that the Magi had approached him prostrating. "Then Herod gathered the chief priests and scribes of the Law, who had studied the books well, and inquired from them where the Christ would be born."

Oh, the divine plan! Just as the Magi were drawn to Him by the things in their hands[5], so He also wanted to draw the Israelites by means of what was in their hands, which are the books of the Law and the prophets, in which they believe. As the Lord said to them, "You search the Scriptures, for in them you think you have eternal life; and these are they which testify of Me." And thus the star was hidden from the Magi until they spread that news. So when the chief priests thoroughly examined it, they acknowledged the truth, so that it would be a testimony against them, saying, "The Christ will be born in Bethlehem." As it is written in the prophet Micah: "And you, O Bethlehem in the land of Judah, are by no means least among the rulers of Judah; for from you shall come a ruler who will shepherd my people Israel."

Look at the clarification of this prophecy. And how Bethlehem was magnified despite its smallness. And why is that? It is because

---

[5] That is, with the knowledge of the stars that they knew, so he showed them a star, a sign of the coming of Christ, to whom be glory. He also wanted to attract the Jews through prophecies.

from it will come forth the ruler who will shepherd Israel. This is the One to whom the prophet David cried out, saying:

"O Shepherd of Israel, who guided Joseph like a flock, look down from Your throne upon Ephraim, Benjamin, and Manasseh. Show us Your power and come to save us." This examination had been ongoing among the Jews diligently, as witnessed by John the Evangelist, saying that some of them said, "This is the Christ," while others said, "Perhaps the Christ will come from Galilee." Did not the scripture say that the Christ will come from the offspring of David, from Bethlehem, the village of David?

Then Herod, out of wickedness, secretly called the Magi and inquired from them the time when the star appeared to them - as a deceitful scheme - and then sent them to Bethlehem, as confirmed by the scribes of the law and the people. He said to them, "Go and search diligently for the child, and when you find Him, inform me so that I may also come and worship Him." It seemed on the surface that he was in agreement with them in everything. However, inwardly, he intended - out of evil and wickedness - to kill Him, thinking that he would be able to do so without anyone knowing. When the Magi heard that the prophets' writings testified that the Christ would be born in Bethlehem, they believed this with great faith. They went seeking the place, and because God wanted to confirm this certainty to them visibly to strengthen their faith, He showed them the star in its original form!! As the Holy Scriptures testified, saying, "When they went, the star they had seen in the east went ahead of them until it stopped over the place where the child was!"

Look now, this star is a sign of God's power that He has shown to them. How it was moving ahead of them, close to them, guiding them until it came and stood over the house where the newborn child was staying. When they saw the star, they rejoiced greatly,

II Glorious Nativity

confirming their faith and dispelling any doubts, so they did not turn right or left, but entered the house where the child was. They did not hesitate at all. When they saw Him with His mother Mary, they knelt down and worshiped Him without any doubt, not seeing around Him any crowds or armies befitting such a great king, for whom they had laboured and travelled this long distance. They did not see any decorations as found in the palaces of the world, but they knelt down to Him, convinced with certainty that He was indeed the Christ, the Saviour of the world, with several signs.

The first being their knowledge of the stars.

The second being the planet that was moving ahead of them and stopping at the place where He was.

The third being the testimony of the prophets as informed by the scribes of the law.

Then they presented Him with gifts of gold, frankincense, and myrrh, as they had narrowed it down to these three types.

The Holy Scriptures did not say that they presented luxurious clothing or anything else typically given to kings, even though they were capable of doing so. Instead, they kept it in their hearts, saying:

If gold precedes, then he is a king.

And if frankincense precedes, then he is a god.

And if myrrh precedes, then it is a sign that he is susceptible to death in a way that death cannot overcome him, because they saw that His kingdom does not end, as the Jews said to the Lord, "We have heard in the Law that the Messiah remains forever."

So the Lord accepted all three types from them.

They believed that he is the Christ the King. And they believed that He is the God, the Saviour of the world. And they believed that He accepts death in a way that cannot be overcome, and the sting of death cannot harm Him, but He is victorious and always will be.

And the angel of the Lord appeared to the Magi at night and instructed them not to return to Herod, but pointed them to go another way to their country, because the Lord guided them to Jerusalem, to be messengers of his noble birth. When they completed that, He commanded them to go in peace in tranquillity and also be messengers for Him in their land.

As for Luke the Evangelist, he mentioned the day of the Lord's birth himself and how He was born in a cave and placed in a manger among the animals, to lead our animalistic minds to the knowledge of His eternal divinity. Then he mentioned how the angel of the Lord appeared to the shepherds at night and announced to them, saying: "Behold, I bring you good news of great joy that will be for all the people, for today in the city of David a Saviour has been born to you; He is the Christ the Lord."

He testified that this joy is universal for all people. And why is that? Because the Saviour is now with humans on earth, to transfer their ranks to the kingdom of heaven.

Suddenly, with the angel, many heavenly hosts appeared praising God and saying, "Glory to God in the highest heaven, and on earth peace to men, and joy among people." So they glorified their heavenly king, for where He is, there His heavenly servants are, and they clarified through this sanctification a unified glorification equal to the Holy Trinity, one in divinity.

They conveyed glory to the Father who is in the highest,

II Glorious Nativity

And to the Son, the King of Peace, who came to earth, through the birth from the Virgin, while in heaven with His divinity, He never ceased.

And the pleasure of the gift of the Holy Spirit, who is to dwell in believers through the second birth.

So the shepherds hurried and witnessed the greatest shepherd of His flock as they were told. Just as the kings also hurried and bowed down to the eternal heavenly king.

John the Evangelist informed us about the various types of wonderful union, saying "The Word became flesh and dwelt among us," meaning that He did not become flesh in terms of impossibility, but in terms of union by saying "and dwelt among us." By this incarnation, it was established that He incarnated from us, then he said: "And we beheld His glory, the glory as of the Only Begotten of the Father, full of grace and truth." Meaning that even though He was born in the flesh and dwelt among us, He did not leave behind the glory of His divinity. Rather, we beheld His glory, full of the grace of His divinity and the truth of His lordship, just as we also beheld Him incarnate. This is the one who was pleased to declare and speak to us with lips.

As for the Apostle Paul, he clarified the meaning by saying "In many ways and various types, God spoke to our fathers by the prophets in ancient times, but in these last days He has spoken to us by His Son." Meaning that He spoke to them in a manner similar to what was intended to be. And here the truth itself is exploited. And when you hear about the last days, do not think of the branches of the world and the perfection of the times, but rather it means the last days of antiquity because their goal is Christ and He is their perfection. Then He began a new law that will not come to an end as befits its establisher.

Then the Apostle explains that He is the special Son born of the eternal Father, without beginning, equal to the Father in essence. He said: "Who has made Him heir of all things, through whom also He made the worlds; who being the brightness of His glory and the express image of His person, and upholding all things by the word of His power."

Look at the power of understanding of the Apostle speaking the truth by the Spirit. How nothing befitting His divinity was left out, as He has appointed it for the incarnate Word, the radiance of the incomprehensible glory of the divinity, His eternal image and the controller of all things and the container of them, and the upholder. The One who specially incarnated for us and was born of the Virgin. Let those who deny the divinity of Christ be ashamed now, and let those who deny His incarnation also be ashamed. I mean Mani and Marcian[6], as the Apostle proclaims His incarnation saying: "He did not take on Himself the nature of angels, but He took on the seed of Abraham" and also said that He became like us in all things except sin.

Blessed are you, O pure Virgin Mary, like the voice of your prophecy saying: "From now on all generations will call me blessed," and truly all blessings and honours have been fulfilled. Because you are called the Mother of the One who existed before all ages, the eternal Son born of the Father without beginning, born of you in the flesh for salvation, O handmaid of the Lord and His witness and mother. You are higher than the heavens, more honourable than the cherubim, and superior to the seraphim, and greater than the ranks of the angelic spirits, and more glorified than the heads of the fathers and the prophets, and more esteemed in dignity than the noble disciples who were sent.

---

6   These heresies apply to the heresy of Jehovah's Witnesses, who deny the divinity of Jesus Christ and that he is the incarnate God.

II Glorious Nativity

You are the pride of our race, in you the virginity boasts, and in you the purity and chastity are honoured. You are the Ark of the Covenant in which the Ten Commandments are inscribed in pure gold embroidery. You are the golden vessel filled with manna hidden and descending from heaven. Pure gold, which is the dignity of the divine nature, is bestowed upon you. You are the rod of Aaron that budded without planting, watering, or tilling. The embodiment of the Word sprouted from you without human sowing. You are the branch that grew from the root of Jesse, and the flower that surpasses all fragrance and perfume.

You are Zion, the mother in whom the Man descended in flesh, the exalted one whom David witnessed.

You are the light cloud upon which the Lord descended to Egypt, as prophesied by Isaiah.

You are the closed gate with the seal of virginity, from which the Lord of glory was born and preserved in virginity forever, as witnessed by the prophet Ezekiel.

You are Zion, in which the Lord God Almighty dwelt, as revealed to Zephaniah.

You are the new heaven from which the Sun of righteousness rose for His worshippers, as announced by Malachi.

Time may limit me to speak of your dignity, you who surpass all dignity. You have been favoured above all creatures, seen and unseen, for the greatness of the dignity of the Lord God who is worshipped, who chose you and was born from you, for the one whom all creation worships in secret is called mother. Therefore, your dignity is great, and your intercession is powerful and abundant in strength and response...!

And you, due to the greatness of your dignity, I am unable to fully praise you to the utmost, so I desire brevity.

Great is the dignity of this honourable feast today, so much so that its commemoration every year brings joy to the heart and delight to the believers in its arrival, because in it the Sun of righteousness was declared to us and shone upon us from the Virgin through the physical birth. We must celebrate it with all purity to partake in the sacred Virgin birth. Learn the virtue of purity and its dignity before God, for from the purity of the Virgin Mary, the mystery of the Lord being incarnated from her is revealed. And it is fitting that she is called mother.

Therefore, we must preserve ourselves to the best of our ability, for He is holy and loves the pure, as it is written, "Be pure, for I am pure," says the Lord. And in the saints, it is fitting as it is written, and for those who keep His commandments, He makes them His dwelling, as witnessed, and He looks upon the humble with eyes of compassion, as spoken by the prophet, saying that those who fear Him and seek Him with honesty, He responds to them, as witnessed, saying: "Ask and you shall receive. Seek and you shall find. Knock and it shall be opened to you."

Let us keep our bodies pure for the Lord who was born of the holy Virgin, and let us keep our souls chaste from impure thoughts for the sake of the dignity of the one who united with His body to bring us closer to the glory of his eternal and incomprehensible divinity. Let us keep our senses unblemished from the sins of sight, hearing, speech, smell, and touch, for the sake of the dignity of the one who sanctified humanity in body, soul, and mind through His union with it.

And because of His boundless humility, He did not hesitate to call us His brothers, as it is written, "I will proclaim your name to my brothers." Therefore, we must understand the dignity that has been bestowed upon us and not take it lightly, striving to excel in all virtues. For whoever has, more will be given, and our celebration should not be marked by worldly revelry and

II Glorious Nativity

excess, but by things befitting the pure, especially since we have observed the fasting discipline leading up to this holy feast. Let us continue in righteousness and the fear of the Lord, reaching out to help the weak as much as we are able. Let us remember those in prison, alleviate the suffering of the needy, make peace with our brothers for the sake of the Lord who came and reconciled the heavenly and earthly realms, drawing us near to Him and making us children of the heavenly Father through the Spirit.

We beseech the Lord Jesus Christ, through the intercession of the Virgin Mary, from whom He was born in the flesh for our salvation, to look upon us with eyes of mercy, forgive our sins, pardon our faults, safeguard the remainder of our lives, grant you all fruitful deeds and radiant crowns, and grant us all a share and portion with all His saints in the eternal kingdom and everlasting life. May He grant rest to the souls of all the baptized through the prayers of the holy apostles, all the martyrs, saints, confessors, and strugglers, and all those who have pleased the Lord with good deeds, now and forever and unto the ages of ages. Amen

III

Glorious Epiphany

Translated from the arabic edition
by Fr Mancarius Awad

In the name of the Father, and of the Son, and of the Holy Spirit, one God, to Him be glory forever. Amen.

The Glorious Feast of Theophany

By the honoured Saint Bulus al-Bushi

His prayers and blessings be with us to the last breath. Amen.

Glory to the source of holiness of the saints who sanctified us through the second birth and the coming of the Holy Spirit when He descended upon the Jordan River in baptism.

Glory to the Eternal One who was born in the flesh to give us spiritual birth through the holy baptism when He was baptized by His servant John and became for us a way to righteousness and guidance.

Glory to the One who humbled Himself and came to the Jordan to fulfil all righteousness, by His righteousness we are justified from sin.

Glory to the One who revealed to us the mystery of the Trinity at the Jordan through His proclamation.[1]

Glory to the One who purified the waters by His presence in them, sanctified the elements, and all the earth by walking upon it.

Glory to You, for You are the Lord Christ who humbled Himself for His love for humanity, and renewed creation through the second birth, the incorruptible One, who is from above, from the Father of lights.

To You I give thanks and praise, O You who removed our shame and made us children of light and day.

---

1 That is, by the appearance of the Holy Trinity.

III Glorious Epiphany

To You I give the greatest and highest praise, O You who are above all authority, power, and dominion.

He chose to humble Himself and be baptized by His servant John, and taught us the path of humility through which we are saved from the snares of the devil.

Grant me knowledge, O You without whom I am unable to do anything, so that I may speak of Your works that surpass all beauty and glory.

Grant me understanding, O giver of all grace, so that I may speak of the plan of Your works that You have declared.

Bestow upon me the gift, O You whose fullness overflows with all spiritual blessings, to proclaim Your humility openly, O Holy One.

Great is the dignity of this glorious feast, beloved brothers, it is called the Feast of Epiphany because in it the mystery of the Trinity is revealed. What was a symbol in the books of the prophets has now been openly revealed to us today, for the Son incarnate has declared all that was hidden, and the example has become truth and perfection, and the things that were hidden from the wise and prudent have now been revealed to infants!

First of all, the greatness of the Holy Trinity, the One in essence, the principle, designer, and perfection of all things, has been revealed to us today. The Son was baptized in the Jordan, the Father in heaven bore witness to Him saying, "This is My beloved Son in whom I am well pleased", and the Holy Spirit appeared in the form of a dove, to indicate that the Spirit is fully consubstantial.

And why did He appear in the form of a dove specifically?!

For the sake of her placidity above all others, as the Lord said, "Be as gentle as doves… and even those upon whom the Spirit descends shall be calm, gentle, and a dwelling place for the Holy Spirit. Walking in the commandments of the Lord as He teaches us, saying, "Learn, not from an angel, nor a prophet, nor a messenger, but from Me alone, for I am gentle and humble in heart, and you will find rest for your souls."

This Holy Trinity in which we believe and in whose name we were baptized, following the example that was in the Jordan as the Lord commanded His pure apostles, saying, "Go and make disciples of all nations, baptizing them in the name of the Father, Son, and Holy Spirit. Whoever believes and is baptized will be saved, but whoever does not believe will be condemned." He also said,

"Truly, truly, I say to you, unless one is born of water and the Spirit, he cannot enter the kingdom of God." Then we understood that this birth is not a physical birth. He said: "Because what is born of the flesh is flesh, and what is born of the Spirit is spirit."

And for the honour of this holy birth, John the Evangelist teaches us, saying, "To those who received Him, He gave them the power to become children of God, not born of blood, nor of the will of the flesh, nor of the will of man, but born of God." This is how we inherit the kingdom of God. For flesh and blood do not inherit it, as the apostle said, "but those who are born of the Spirit." Therefore, when the Lord wanted to declare Himself to the people after thirty years of His birth in the flesh, He began first with the declaration of the Holy Trinity one in divinity, then showed us the complete way above all perfection. I mean the manner of the second birth, the beginning of faith, and the pledge of the inheritance of sonship through which redemption and freedom were obtained.

Come now, O you four Evangelists, the four rivers of life flowing from the fountain of the intellectual paradise, who watered the

III Glorious Epiphany

whole world and informed us of the dignity of this glorious feast today.

When the Evangelist tells us about the announcement of repentance, saying: "In those days John the Baptist came preaching in the wilderness of Judea, saying, 'Repent, for the kingdom of God is at hand,' for this is He who was spoken of by the prophet Isaiah, saying: 'The voice of one crying in the wilderness: Prepare the way of the Lord, make His paths straight.'" This means that John came from the wilderness before the Lord, as written by Luke the Evangelist about him, "He was in the wilderness until the day of his manifestation to Israel." And the word of God came to John the son of Zacharias in the wilderness, and all the surrounding country of the Jordan went out to him, preaching a baptism of repentance for the forgiveness of sins. But why did he not come to other places, but only to the surrounding country of the Jordan? That is because it was intended for the baptism of the Lord, who came for it to the Jordan River. He mentioned in his preaching that he preached with a baptism of repentance for the forgiveness of sins, to abolish the sprinkling of hyssop and the ashes of the heifer used by the children of Israel. Those which were not mentioned as being for the forgiveness of sins, but for the purification from touching the bones of the dead or a leper. Those who have no sin.

Likewise, this is what John and the Jews say for the sake of purification, because this will be abolished when it is not the goal but only a symbol of what is intended to be. So John was a mediator between the old and the new, as the Lord says: "The Law and the Prophets were until John." And he is like Elijah who is to come as prophesied by Malachi, and he is greater than a prophet as testified by the Lord, and he is a messenger as he testified about himself to the Jews, saying: "I am not the Christ, but I am a messenger before Him." And he is an angel on earth as prophesied by Isaiah, saying: "Behold, I send My messenger before Your face, who will prepare Your way before You." For the forgiveness of sins, this forgiveness that has come to us with the proclamation of the Lord.

And for this saying, there is also another ecclesiastical interpretation, meaning the voice crying in the wilderness is the good news of the pure apostles in the corners of the earth to the nations, because these nations were wilderness and desolate, devoid of hearing the word of faith. He said: "Prepare the way of the Lord," meaning if they believe, they will prepare the way for the Lord to dwell in them with the Spirit, as it is written, "I will dwell in them and walk among them," says the Lord.

He said, "And make His paths straight," meaning if He dwells in them. For the Spirit guides them to make the paths of the Lord straight, without crookedness.

He said, "Every valley shall be filled, and every mountain and hill shall be brought low." By valleys, he means the nations who were devoid of the knowledge of God and had fallen down to the abyss and descended into the pit of destruction through the deception of the devil, the worship of idols, and other wicked deeds. So they were filled with spiritual knowledge through faith until they became teachers and interpreters of the words of the prophets and apostles! By hills He is referring to the hills where the leaders of the Jews and the forces of the devils fell, as the Prophet says: "We destroy every high thing that exalts itself above the knowledge of God."

As for the Jews who remained unbelievers, the kingdom and leadership were taken away from them, and the priesthood was invalidated for them because their priesthood is only complete in the temple of Solomon. And the protection of the prophets was removed from them because their goal was the incarnation of the Messiah. Then the Jewish people were scattered in the corners of the earth under the hands of foreign kings who ruled over them forever without a covenant. As for the devils, He humiliated them by the appearance of His hypostasis openly, as the Prophet says, and He subjected everything opposed to Him under His feet.

He said: "The rough places will be made smooth and the rugged paths will be made straight," meaning the rough paths of the nations and the harshness of their characters became smooth and easy with the evangelical message. And so the hard, wild, and rough hearts softened with discipline and teaching, and submitted to obedience.

He said: "And all flesh shall see the salvation of God," meaning those who walk in this straight path of any race, they witness the salvation of God, because the Prophet says all flesh, not specifying Jews or Gentiles, but making all in the faith one.

Mark specifically begins the Gospel with the baptism of the Lord by John, saying: "The beginning of the Gospel of Jesus Christ, the Son of God," because the meaning of the word Gospel is the good news, meaning that the beginning of the good news of our Lord Jesus Christ, the Son of God, was proclaimed to humans since the baptism, as Peter the Apostle mentioned in the Acts, saying that it began from the baptism by John because the Lord stayed thirty years on earth without manifesting Himself openly and the people did not know Him until the time of the baptism. Then after the baptism He began to teach and make disciples, and for this reason Mark the Evangelist made it the beginning of the good news and left out what Matthew and Luke mentioned about the birth and other matters, aiming at the appearance of the Lord and making that the opening of his Gospel, because in it the mystery of the Trinity appeared openly and it became the beginning of faith in the holy baptism, because the Lord became an example and a way leading to eternal life. And in this way, He gave examples and teachings to the teachers of the covenant, as the noble apostles who laid the foundation of the covenant in the book of the Didache said: "No one should be ordained to the priesthood who is under thirty years old, even if he is a knowledgeable, chaste, and righteous man known for his righteousness" because our Lord Jesus Christ Himself was baptized and began to teach us according to this example. But the apostles preserved this example of baptism for three excellent reasons: the first is to preserve the Trinity for thirteen complete decades, the second is that at its perfection, a person completes dignity, stature, and intellect, and the third is that natural desire erupts in a person around the age of eighteen and is tested until the age of thirty, which is the power of youthful heat. So, if he is found during this period to be pious, chaste, worshipful of God, avoiding faults, he is deserving of the priesthood and suitable for it. Because the initial education became a preserver for him with the help of the Lord.

Then John began to warn the people and teach them an excellent teaching, strong without flattery or fear, rebuking the hypocrites and those who resemble them, saying, "You brood of vipers, who warned you to flee from the coming wrath, meaning the judgment of God for all." He said, "Produce fruit in keeping with repentance. And do not say, 'We have Abraham as our father,' for God is able to raise up children for Abraham from these stones." By stones, he meant the nations who used to worship idols made of stones and others, as David said, "Those who make them will be like them, and so will all who trust in them." But those who became children of Abraham are those who walked in the righteousness of faith in our Lord Jesus Christ, as the apostle Paul said.

Then John began to teach the tax collectors and soldiers along with all the people openly, without fear or terror, to the extent that they all thought he was the Christ when they saw his teaching, which was authoritative, and his warning about the baptism of repentance for the forgiveness of sins, and his leaving aside the deceitful ways. But John answered them, saying, "I am not the Christ, but the one who comes after me, the one who existed before me in divinity," and he revealed His divinity and humanity together with this word.

He said, "I am not worthy to untie the straps of His sandals," meaning the law of the Lord that he established and walked in first, and he commanded us to follow in his footsteps, as the apostle testified, saying, "And with your feet fitted with the readiness that comes from the gospel of peace" (Ephesians 6:15).

He said, "He will baptize you with the Holy Spirit and fire." Meaning that all things are under Him, and He is perfection, and that is why He is the one who baptizes all because He is the doer in all. Unlike John with water for repentance, Christ's baptising will be by the action of the Holy Spirit, who has the power to sanctify and purify, and with the fire of His worship, which is from the heat of faith, and it has the power of forgiveness of sins and all the faults that occur after baptism, as the Lord said, "I have come to bring fire on the earth, and how I wish it were already kindled." This fire truly ignited in the saints until they completed their striving with strength and righteous effort.

"The one with the winnowing fork in His hand will clear His threshing floor, gathering the wheat into His barn and burning up the chaff with unquenchable fire." Here, it is evident to all people that Christ, who appeared in the flesh, is God over all by saying that He baptizes with the Holy Spirit. It is known that the Lord did not baptize anyone with His hand, as John the Evangelist testified, but he is the one who acts and sanctifies all with the power of His divinity present everywhere. This is further emphasized by his statement that He will gather His wheat, complete them, and keep them in His barn, which is His eternal kingdom. As for the people who are like chaff and straw, and have turned away with all their sinful desires, He will throw them into the unquenchable fire of hell to teach them that He justifies, condemns, raises to the kingdom, and casts into hell.

John completed the warning diligently, not compromising, teaching and weeping, and turning souls straight to the Lord, as his father Zechariah prophesied, saying: "And you, child, will be called a prophet of the Most High; for you will go on before the Lord to prepare the way for him, to give his people the knowledge of salvation through the forgiveness of their sins."

The angel Gabriel testified about him, saying: "He will turn many of the children of Israel to the Lord their God. He will go on before the Lord in the spirit and power of Elijah to turn the hearts of the fathers to their children and the disobedient to the wisdom of the righteous, to make ready a people prepared for the Lord."

When all this was completed, the Holy Scriptures say that Jesus came from Galilee to the Jordan to be baptized by John.

Oh, the humility that cannot be measured, and human language cannot translate: How is it that the Lord, to whom all humans come, as it is written, comes to the Jordan and does not object to it?! The source of Holiness came to be baptized by the one whom he sanctified, blessed, chose, and gave the gift of his Holy Spirit, and sent him as a herald before him, not because he needed it, but for us who are in need!!! Not even for the acceptance of the Holy Spirit, because He is eternal in the one divine essence!! But to give us the gift of the Holy Spirit through baptism in His name, the Holy One. He purified the waters by His descent into them and sanctified them, and He also purified us by the descent of the Holy Spirit descending upon us.

And what does the divine scripture say?!

III Glorious Epiphany

John said that he refused and excused himself, saying "I am the one who needs to rely on You." He means, You don't need anything from this, because You are the righteous one alone, but I and those like me from all humans who are under condemnation need to rely on You, the giver of talents to all who approach him, and the sanctifier in all sanctifications, and from you specifically they are sanctified and blessed. O Holy One, we need to be sanctified by You and not by anyone else but You, O one without whom no one can do anything of grace, O righteous one who alone is without fault, we need to be justified by You so that we may be saved from the condemnation that came to us from the first Adam. We need You to tear up our book of sins, we need You to give us life after death when You send Your voice so that the dead hear and the righteous and the wicked rise together, we need You to show us mercy in Your feared judgment, we need You to save us from eternal punishment and give us life in the everlasting kingdom, You do not need our worship but we need your lordship and mercy.

John was amazed by the humility of the Lord and excused himself saying: "How can You come to me when I am the one who needs to rely on you!!" So He answered him saying: "Allow it, because this is how it is fitting for us to fulfil all righteousness."

Leave now this objection and excuse, because you do not know the power of My divine plan. As He said to Peter when he refused have his feet washed: "What I do, you do not know now but you will know it later", and when Peter did not find an excuse, he let Christ wash his feet. And so it happened in the case of John also by saying "allow it", meaning leave this dispute and do what I command you to do because this is how it is fitting for us to fulfil all righteousness, and the meaning of all righteousness is that the Creator visited His creation Himself and entrusted it to Himself to justify us from condemnation. The Creator did not reject what His hands made, because only the Creator can fix His creation's corruption, and He did not just entrust it to Himself but became an example and a way leading to eternal life, as He said "I am the way, the truth, and the life." Through Him we have salvation and forgiveness of sins. And through Him we have progressed because He is above all holiness, as for John, when he could not excuse himself and found no way out, he began to submit to his master's command.

When the Lord was baptized, He rose up immediately from the water, showing us the speed of His care for us, and the heavens opened to Him because He is the owner of all things. The Spirit of God appeared descending like a dove towards Him to show that the Spirit is fully of one essence, and He was declared for the Son's declaration to be working in all sanctifications. Since the Holy Spirit was not incarnate, He appeared in the form of a dove, unlike any other bird in its placidity. And a voice from heaven said, "This is My beloved Son, in whom I am well pleased," and this feast is called the Epiphany as mentioned earlier. Because in it appeared the mystery of the Holy Trinity, the Son in the Jordan, the Father testifying to Him, and the Holy Spirit descending upon Him. Why did He not descend upon the Lord while He was in the Jordan River? So that it would not be thought that He descended upon John the Baptist, because his name was well known. Therefore, when the Lord ascended from the water and separated from John, He descended upon Him specifically, and although the Spirit was with Him, He remained in the unity of the Godhead, one in essence, and He did this so that everyone baptized by this example in the name of the Holy Trinity would receive the gift of the Holy Spirit, because the Lord became an example for us in everything.

John the Evangelist made the opening of his Gospel about the eternal birth that has no beginning, saying: "In the beginning was the Word, and the Word was with God, and the Word was God." So when He came, He did not neglect the plan of the

III Glorious Epiphany

incarnation and the sacred baptism for its sake, but He confirmed it by the descent of the Spirit over the Jordan and the statement of John the Baptist that he saw and testified that this is the Son of God. Not only that but He demonstrated and confirmed it further for us specifically with Nicodemus. The Lord said to Nicodemus that you must be born from above, because what is born of the flesh is flesh, and what is born of the Spirit is spirit, and He said that whoever is not born of water and the Spirit cannot see the kingdom of God. This is what renewed us and made us children of the Father in eternal life, as the Apostle says that sometimes through the washing of the second birth and the renewal of the gift of the Holy Spirit, meaning that the Spirit that was taken from Adam at the fall, He renewed it in us through baptism freely by His grace. He said: "He poured it out on us abundantly through Jesus Christ our Saviour, so that we might be justified by His grace and become heirs of the hope of eternal life."

Therefore, my beloved, the dignity of this feast is very great, and we must honour it because in it, the mystery of the Trinity was declared to us. Today, the Son has given us the authority to be born from above and become children of God the Father through the Spirit. "The Spirit Himself also bears witness with our spirit that we are children of God" (Romans 8:16).

Today the Lord crushed the head of the dragon on the waters as David prophesied. Today the Son freed us from our bitter bondage and we have become free when He bestowed upon us the gift of His Holy Spirit, the same Spirit that he took from our father Adam when he ate from the tree of transgression. Today all what was written in the book of Joel is fulfilled, that "I will pour out my Spirit on all people, says the Lord". Let us now celebrate a pure and holy feast as is fitting, for in it the Lord has purified us by the coming of His Holy Spirit and given us a new birth. And there is no seed that will perish as before, but rather that which will not perish for the inheritance of the eternal kingdom, revealed to us with no end. And today we hear the loud voice saying: Prepare the way of the Lord and make His paths straight. And if this has come through John and He cried out bodily in the ears, our pure apostolic fathers have completed it ecclesiastically in the proclamation of the good news and the building of the church, as mentioned earlier. For he remains to this day standing firm, becoming spiritual to us, crying out in the ears of our souls that have become like a barren wilderness devoid of righteous deeds, neglecting them. He commands us to make way for the Lord to dwell in us by the Spirit when we keep His commandments, as He said: "If anyone loves me, He will keep my word, and my Father will love Him, and We will come to Him and make our home with Him" (John 14:23).

What could be more noble than the fact that the lowly earthly human becomes a dwelling place for the great heavenly God, carrying out His commandments. Then the valleys within that soul, which were filled with weakness of heart, lack of trustworthiness, and hopelessness, become filled with faith, strength, and righteous hope in God. The mountains within it humble the peaks of pride, arrogance, and disobedience to God's law, and become humble for the Lord who humbled Himself for us. Submitting to His law with love and diligence, keeping His commandments with delight, so that the soul that was once rough in its ways becomes easy to guide, and the one that was initially wild and harsh in temperament becomes gentle and easy in its behaviour. Thus, the law of the Spirit is engraved and imprinted in them, not on tablets of stone but on soft, fleshy hearts, as the apostle says. And so, every human witnesses this work of God's salvation. We must remember the covenant we made with the Lord at the time of baptism, following the apostolic commands to resist the devil and all his works, to follow the law of the Lord and all His deeds. And if we have stumbled and acted contrary to this, let us renew ourselves with the fire of repentance from the Spirit. Let us rise from our fall and turn away from the path of destruction. For the Lord calls us through the mouth of the prophet Isaiah, saying: "Return to me, and I will return to you," says the Lord. Even if your sins are as scarlet, they shall be as white as snow; even if they are red as crimson, they shall be like wool. If we neglect this, the apostle's words will be fulfilled upon us: "There is no covenant or faithfulness for them." This word is specifically addressed to the believers, those who know that the judgment of God is death for those who practice these abominations, not only doing them themselves but also approving of those who practice them (Romans 1:31).

Now we return to the Lord with pure repentance to cleanse ourselves from these abominations and wash away the filth of its defilement. For the Lord instructs us through the mouth of the prophet Isaiah, saying: "Wash yourselves, make yourselves clean; remove the evil of your deeds from before my eyes; cease to do evil" (Isaiah 1:16). The prophet rebukes a people who persist in their sins and ignorance, saying: "Woe to those who rise early in the morning to run after strong drink, who tarry late into the evening as wine inflames them!" (Isaiah 5:11). This refers to those who are careless in defiling their souls with sins from their youth to the fullness of their lives, only to be overtaken by the evening which is death, where there is no more work and no repentance is accepted. Let us strive now in doing good deeds to the best of our abilities while we still have time and opportunity before death overtakes us, so that we may find assistance from Him, obtain His mercy, and may the Lord protect us all from the snares of the enemy and his traps, and prepare us to hear that joyful voice saying: "Come, O blessed of my Father, inherit the kingdom prepared for you from the foundation of the world". Through the intercession of our Lady, the holy Virgin Mary, the

Mother of Salvation, and the intercession of the righteous Saint John the Baptist, and the intercessions of our holy apostles, martyrs, and saints. Amen

IV

Palm Sunday

Translated from the arabic edition
by Fr Mancarius Awad

In the name of the Father, the Son, and the Holy Spirit, the one God to whom be glory. Amen.

Homily on Palm Sunday

By the honoured Saint Bulus al-Bushi

May his prayers and blessings be with us until the last breath Amen.

Great are your works, O Lord, the glorified God, in your saints. Human tongue cannot describe the depth of your works or interpret the beauty of Your magnificent understanding. Yet, I send glory, honour, reverence, and worship to Your revered name, O Christ of glory and majesty, and I ask You to open my mouth to speak of the splendour of Your glory.

Grant me understanding, O Christ, who gave praise to children so that I may praise with them the greatness of Your splendour. Grant me to say, O Emmanuel our God, so that I may cry out with those who went out with palm branches to meet You and say: "Blessed is He who comes in the name of the Lord", and he is coming soon. Glory to you in the highest above and on earth below. I sing today with the prophet David and cry out saying: "Declare to the Lord His deeds and wonders among mankind."

You declared Yourself to Your creation, O Christ the Lord, after Your baptism in the Jordan River. And You showed Your works to Your creation when You appeared incarnate according to Your will, and You showed works befitting Your divinity, so that everyone may know that You are a God incarnate because of Your works that were done with power and authority, calling the Gentiles to be preachers, and You granted them all wisdom and understanding!!

You turned water into wine at the wedding in Cana of Galilee by Your blessing. And when they asked You for healing, You

IV Palm Sunday

cleansed the leper by Your will. By Your name, You calmed the sea in front of Your disciples and in one catch, the two boats were filled with fish. With a word from Your mouth, You healed the centurion's son. You raised Peter's mother-in-law from her fever. By touching the edge of Your garment, You healed the woman with the issue of blood. You raised Jairus' daughter. You called Lazarus from the tomb after four days. You raised the widow's daughter in Nain!! You drove out the demons from the possessed people, and the paralysed carried their beds by Your command, and You forgave their sins. You healed various diseases by the power of Your divinity, and You showed mercy and acceptance to sinners and tax collectors. You gave sight to the blind, hearing to the deaf, extended hands to the mute, and showed compassion to those who were like sheep without a shepherd. You spoke in many parables for our salvation, and You satisfied thousands of people with a little bread. You walked on the liquid water in its nature, which You made firm under Peter Your disciple's feet. The stormy winds were calmed at Your command!!

And the glory of Your divinity was manifested in front of Your apostles, and coins were taken out of the mouth of a fish in the depths of the sea. You forgave the sinful woman who anointed Your feet with perfume, and the fig tree that did not bear fruit withered. You guided and led the lost, and showed patience and compassion to the disobedient people. You lifted and glorified those who obeyed Your command, and announced the renewed life and the promised kingdom. You warned about the eternal punishment and hell prepared for sinners, and spoke and warned about Your second coming and terrifying judgment. You instructed and preached everything that leads to our benefit. You prohibited and warned about different types of sins!

And when the Lord God completed all this glory, He wanted to fulfill the rest of what the prophets had foretold by completing the goal of salvation through His life-giving death, as He had informed His pure apostles. This is the one who tears apart the book of our sins. With His voice, rocks split, tombs open, the dead rise, elements tremble, He goes to imprisoned souls, breaks iron barriers, shatters bronze doors, and says to those in captivity, "Come out," and to those in darkness, "Look," as the prophet Isaiah had foretold. He rescues those in hell and opens paradise, nullifies the pains of death with His holy resurrection, confirms our hope in the resurrection, and raises our human body, which was once in the dust, to the highest heavens above all rulers and powers.

Then He sends the gift of His Holy Spirit upon His pure apostles to proclaim it to the ends of the earth. The completion of all this was only through His life-giving sufferings!

At that time he went up to Jerusalem saying: The Son of Man must be delivered into the hands of the nations and be killed and rise on the third day. He said this openly and his ascent to Jerusalem was on Sunday the ninth day of the lunar month, on the fourteenth of which the lamb that the Lord made on Thursday of that year was slaughtered. For it is written in the Law that the Lord spoke to Moses in Egypt saying: Thus spoke the congregation of the children of Israel, that each of them should buy a lamb according to the number of his household and it should be without blemish and kept by them from the tenth to the fourteenth of the month to be slaughtered in the evening... Therefore the Lord went up to Jerusalem to be there on the tenth of the month, the day on which the lamb is kept with them as commanded in the Law, because He is the true lamb without blemish as prophesied by Isaiah!! He is the lamb of God who carries the sins of the world as witnessed by John. He is without blemish, complete and present in every time. For the lamb without blemish was not present at any time of the year except when it was present, it is present in winter, spring, summer, and autumn. This example symbolizes that the Lord was not there before, but He exists in all ages and remains preserved by His will in Jerusalem, the place where the plan is completed, from Monday the tenth of the month to Friday the fourteenth of it. And it is the day on which the Passover is slaughtered.

The Lord first resembled this example of the lamb, then gave His apostles until now the completion, which is His holy Body and His precious Blood saying: "This is the new covenant that you shall make in remembrance until He comes" (1 Cor 11: 25,26). I mean that the old has passed away because it was only an example for the new covenant, which is the goal.

His ascent to Jerusalem was humble as befits all His actions!! Riding on a donkey as it is written: Fear not, daughter of Zion, behold, Your king is coming to You, humble and mounted on a donkey, on a colt, the foal of a beast of burden. In another sense, the Law says about the clean animal and the unclean animal as follows: Every animal that does not chew the cud or has a split hoof is unclean. As for the camel, it chews the cud, but its hoof is not split, so it is unclean. This is an example of the Jews because they acknowledge the old Law, which testifies to the new covenant but they did not accept it, therefore, they are unclean. Just as the camel's hoof we find in it a sign of being divided, and from the bottom, it is round and undivided, therefore, the Law says it is unclean. Likewise, the Jews have the old covenant. And in it is a sign of the testimony of the prophets symbolizing the new covenant, yet they did not accept it. They are unclean as they did not accept the two laws. Because the first did not have the goal, but the second has completeness and perfection.

As for the pig, the Law said that it is cloven-footed, but it does not chew the cud, so it is impure. This is an example of one who accepts the old and the new. But he did not act upon it and he is going against the commandment. He accepts the law in words and nullifies it in deeds. The Apostle Jacob says that faith without works is dead. Therefore, he remains cursed as long as he is in transgression, but if he repents and acts according to the commandment, he will be forgiven. For the blessed seed in the richness of faith is present in him as the Prophet Isaiah said, but here we see faith lacking from both sides because he does not chew the cud, and he is cloven-footed. This is an example of nations who worship idols, because they do not know the old or the new. They do not understand anything from the commandments in order to act upon them. These nations, it is a mystery that the Lord put His name upon them by faith and justifies them freely!!

And just as the Lord sent His disciples to untie the donkey and the colt, the son of the donkey, which were tied outside the road, and because they were animals, they did not intend anything from themselves, likewise He sent His disciples to preach to the nations and untie them from the devil's grip, where they did not understand. This is because their minds were beastly, and they were outside the path of righteousness. But God knew that they would accept the truth and submit to faith once they knew it. And just as the prophecy witnessed our Lord riding the donkey, so did the prophecies of the prophets come true with the entry of the nations into faith. "As it is written in Hosea, I will call them My people, who were not My people, and her beloved, who was not beloved. And in the place where it was said to them, 'You are not my people,' there they will be called sons of the living God" (Romans 9:25). David says, "Praise the Lord, all you nations; extol Him, all you peoples." And Isaiah says, "In that day the Root of Jesse will stand as a banner for the peoples; the nations will rally to him, and His resting place will be glorious." And many prophets have prophesied such things.

IV Palm Sunday

The evangelist said, "Those who went ahead and those who followed shouted, 'Hosanna!' 'Blessed is He who comes in the name of the Lord!' 'Blessed is the coming kingdom of our father David!' 'Hosanna in the highest heaven!'" (Mark 11:9). The interpretation of 'Hosanna' in Hebrew means 'save us.'

He said: "And the people spread their cloaks on the road," and this refers to the righteous martyrs who sacrificed their bodies patiently to confess His holy name!! He said, "And the people cut branches from the trees and spread them on the road." And this example was made by the saints, the righteous people of faith who adorned the road before the Lord with virtuous deeds!! He said: "And when He entered Jerusalem, the whole city was stirred," meaning from witnessing the strength and praising of the multitudes with loud voices.

Then He entered the temple and began to drive out those who were selling cattle, sheep, doves, and money changers, to teach us that the house of God should not be filled with worldly distractions that contradict true worship, but rather should be like the heavens for praise, sanctification, and prayers, as He taught them saying, "My house shall be called a house of prayer."

They brought to Him in the temple the blind and the lame, and He healed them to confirm the teaching with the power of signs and wonders. Then He gave understanding to the children so that they may praise Him, causing the elders of the people whose hearts were blinded to the truth to weep with them, as well as causing the ignorant to be amazed and the weak to be strengthened, and the powerful to be humbled. As for the Pharisees who loved glory, and the chief priests who exalted themselves, they envied Him because of the abundance of praises and the crowds flocking to Him, and they said to Him in anger, "Do you not hear what these are saying?!" He reminded them of the scriptures gently, like a good and compassionate teacher, saying, "Have you not read that out of the mouths of infants and nursing babies you have prepared praise?!" But due to their stubbornness and hardness of heart, they persisted in their wickedness, saying among themselves, "Do you not see that you know nothing. The whole world has followed Him, not only envying Him for the people's celebration, but also for His own disciples when they glorified Him." So they said to Him cunningly and enviously, "Teacher, rebuke your disciples so that they may be silent." He declared to them what was intended to happen, saying, "Truly I tell you, if these were silent, the stones would cry out!"

By stones He is referring to the nations whose hearts were stony with idol worship, as mentioned earlier, they became successors to the disciples in faith. They became speakers of faith and teachers of allegiance. They interpreted the words of the messengers and prophets, and built on their foundation sacred and noble stones!! Among them were holy martyrs, and righteous virtuous ones beyond count. Truly, they adorned the straight path before the Lord with every kind of goodness and beauty, and their memory remains eternal. We must find their ways, be inspired by their good deeds, as the apostle said, excel in noble talents. We follow their footsteps and emulate their ways. Even if we cannot shed the garment that is the body's sacrifice unto death in the name of the Lord, let us not give up or be idle, but rather lay branches of trees before Him on the path He showed us, which is the practice of virtue according to our strength as long as we have time and opportunity. Let us cry out before Him, not with sophisticated words, but with the voices of children, with humble hearts devoid of evil and deceit.

As the apostle teaches us, saying: "Do not be children in your thinking, but be children in evil." Let us follow the footsteps of the apostle, cry out and say: "Blessed is He who comes, and is about to come in the name of the Lord, blessed in the

IV Palm Sunday

highest, on earth the eternal Lord King." Let us show mercy to our brothers so that the Lord may have mercy on us, let us repent of our injustice and violation so that we may hear the voice with Zacchaeus saying "today salvation has come to this house." Let us leave the village to meet Him, which is to depart from worldly matters, and let us not leave idle, but leave with dignity, diligence, and in our hands the palm branches, which is the practice of virtue that always grows upwards to be accepted by Him. Let us delight in His glory, as written in the prophets, "come out from among them and be separate, and I will welcome you, says the Lord, and I will be a father to you, and you shall be sons and daughters to me."

Let us keep our bodies pure, for they are the temples of God; and our souls clean, for they are His image. Let us harmonize with the mental forces in spiritual worship. Let us make peace with one another so that the Lord may grant us the peace He gave to His pure apostles. Let us ascend with Him from Jericho to Jerusalem, which is the ascent of the mind from the world of sins to the elevation to heavenly Jerusalem, the city of the pure, where the eternal King Christ the Lord dwells with all His saints. Let us implore Him with the blind man who was sitting on the road from Jericho to Jerusalem, which is the path of the present life, we ask Him to enlighten the eyes of our hearts and help us to work according to His will, and spare us the trials of the enemy, forgive our past sins, guard our lives, forgive us our mistakes, and grant us mercy in His awesome judgment, and make us worthy to hear that voice filled with glory and joy saying: Come, O blessed of my Father, inherit the kingdom prepared for you from the foundation of the world, through the intercession of our Lady, the holy Virgin Mary, the Mother of Salvation, and all the pure apostles, martyrs, and righteous saints. Amen.

V

Crucifixion

Translated from the arabic edition
by Fr Mancarius Awad

In the name of the Father, the Son, and the Holy Spirit, the one God, to Him be glory forever. Amen.

Homily on the Crucifixion

By the Honourable Saint Bulus al-Bushi.

May his prayers and blessings be with us until the last breath Amen.

O Christ, who conquered Satan by the Cross, save us - we, Your faithful people in Your name - from the trials of the enemy, by the power of Your divine nature that reigns over all.

O Lord, who tore apart the book of our sins by the Cross. O Holy Lord, forgive our sins with Your indescribable compassion.

O Lord, who split the rocks, opened the tombs, and raised the dead, soften our stony hearts and revive our minds dead in sin, for You are the giver of eternal life.

O Lord, who illuminated the depths of darkness, enlighten the darkness of our hearts with the light of Your wondrous glory, grant me, the unworthy, understanding to speak in secret of Your providence.

O Lord, who overcame the strength of the mighty by weakness, grant strength to my mind to speak of the extent of your life-giving suffering. Grant me knowledge, O one who freely gave salvation through Your Cross to those who were in the bondage of corruption, humiliated since the beginning of the world, and to all creation forever and the end of time, so that we may know of Your love for our kind, and how You sacrificed Yourself for us out of love from the death that interrogated us. You who surpassed all pains. You who gives life to all flesh for our sake before accepting death. You who exceeding all expectations, for us humans, came down to the Cross.

V Crucifixion

Wonderful are Your works, O Lord, and very deep are Your ways, and Your effects are unknown, O Master, and Your paths are unsearchable, O Holy One.

You, by the holy Cross, showed victory, and by Your life-giving death, You trampled the destructive death and nullified its sting, which is the power of sin, and You freed us, the prisoners of death, meaning that the holy Cross conquered and defeated the invincible, the devil and his soldiers.

The holy body, free from sin, killed sin and destroyed it, and freed us from its bondage. The Lamb without blemish who was led to the slaughter, as the word of the Prophet Isaiah, and became a complete sacrifice and by His offering perfected those who are sanctified forever.

The perfection and completeness of the New Covenant, we have been delivered from the bondage of Pharaoh once and for all, who is the eternal devil, because when God struck Pharaoh and the Egyptians with painful blows, Pharaoh did not release the people, but his heart hardened as God said to Moses His servant, "This final blow will be the one after which he will let you go and you will be delivered from the bondage of Pharaoh forever." So now the people were instructed to each buy a lamb according to the size of their household and it should be a perfect lamb without blemish. They were to keep it from the tenth day of the month until the fourteenth day, then slaughter it in the evening and roast it over the fire, sprinkling its blood on the doorposts and lintels of their houses. They were to eat it quickly with their loins girded, sandals on their feet, and staffs in their hands, for it is the Lord's Passover. Whatever is left over should be burned. Its bones should not be broken, for on this night I will pass through Egypt and strike down every firstborn, but when I see the blood on your door, I will pass over you and the destroyer will not touch you." The interpretation in the article on Palm

Sunday is that the lamb symbolizes Christ and that He is perfect in every time. He entered Jerusalem on the tenth day of the month and stayed until the fourteenth, when the Passover lamb is slaughtered. He first performed the example and then gave his messengers the perfect Passover, which is his body and blood.

As for the interpretation of the rest of the chapter, when God struck Pharaoh and the Egyptians with the nine painful blows, and Pharaoh did not release the people, God said to Moses, "This final blow will be the one after which he will let you go." Similarly, when Christ came to earth to save His people, He struck with the devil and his soldiers painful blows, such as His baptism in the Jordan River, the voice of the Father to Him, and the descent of the Holy Spirit upon Him. Just as Pharaoh, when he was in pain from the blow and it was removed from him, his heart hardened again and he did not let the people go, so in every work that the Lord does fitting His divinity at that time, the devil says, "This is the Christ, the Saviour of the world who has come..." and he suffers greatly and is very sad... then the Lord does something fitting for humanity at that time, because He is the incarnate God and can do both, and He is one doer without division.

The voice of the Father came, testifying that He is His beloved Son, and the Spirit descended upon Him saying, "Truly, this is the Christ, the Lord, the only begotten Son." The devil was greatly saddened, and at that time the Lord went up to the mountain and fasted for forty days and forty nights, to teach us to follow in His footsteps. Satan approached Him to tempt Him, and said to Him, "If you are the Son of God, command these stones to become bread." He said this because of the voice that testified that He is the beloved Son of God. But the Lord did not do as he desired, but rebuked him and cast him away. Likewise, He did all His miracles with authority, such as cleansing the lepers, casting out demons, raising the dead, feeding the crowds

V Crucifixion

with little bread, walking on water, calming the winds, healing various diseases, raising the paralysed, opening the eyes of the blind, and the ears of the deaf, and more. Not only that, but He also gave His apostles the power to perform these miracles in His holy name, saying, "Heal the sick. Cleanse the lepers. Cast out demons. Raise the dead. Freely you have received, freely give."

These were the painful blows to Satan and his soldiers when they learned that the Christ, whom the prophets had foretold, had come, and that He had performed deeds befitting His divinity. How the Lord gave power to His apostles - who were weak people - to perform miracles in His name, because they can only be done in the name of the God who has power over all things!

So Satan was troubled by this and greatly disturbed. Whenever he saw Him fasting, praying, and doing things befitting humanity, he found a loophole and rest, like Pharaoh in that time, and he persisted in his evil ways. Because of his arrogance, he did not consider Him well, because he was cruel and wicked, and his fall was deadly.

The Lord had kept him for the final blow, in which the true Passover was enacted, which was an example for Him. When the Lord made the example and gave His apostles perfection, He informed them of His life-giving sufferings at that time, and that He was sacrificing Himself for them and for all, not for Himself but for us, for the forgiveness of our sins and the acquisition of eternal life.

Oh, the abundant mercy and available love. He who said, "There is no greater love than this, that a man should lay down his life for his friends." He also testified, saying, "For God so loved the world that He gave His only begotten Son, that whoever believes in Him should not perish but have eternal life."

And on that night when He enacted the Passover and surrendered Himself to the crucifixion, He completed everything that was written for Him.

It is commanded in the law that they shall smear the blood on the doorposts, both upper and lower, and also on the sides, as a sign of the holy cross. It is said: "The lamb shall be eaten roasted by fire," meaning the fire of the Holy Spirit by which we have accepted it in faith. It is said that it shall be eaten in the evening, for the Lord stayed on the cross until the evening. It is said that your loins shall be girded, meaning to worship Him with diligence and love, as commanded in the Gospel. And Peter says, "Gird up the loins of your minds and be sober," meaning not only to gird the body but also the heart. It is said that your sandals shall be on your feet, meaning that we must partake of it while walking in the straight path, obeying and acting according to the Gospel commandments, as the apostle says: "Having shod your feet with the preparation of the gospel of peace" (Ephesians 6:15).

It is said that your staff shall be in your hand, meaning that we should hold on to the staff of strength, which is a sign of kingship, and if we take it with complete reverence, we shall inherit eternal life through it.

It is said that you shall eat it quickly because it is the Lord's Passover. This means that we should not be negligent but diligent, acting and obeying, knowing that there is nothing greater than it, for it is the Lord's Passover by which He passed over His people, meaning He saved them.

It is said that whatever is left of it, eat it, meaning its remnants. It is said that what is not eaten, burn it with fire, exempting its horns, hooves, hair, and skin to be burned by fire. And by remnants that are eaten, it means the special and general ones, such as the verses of the Lord, His wonders, and the manifestation

V Crucifixion

of His divinity, which are not eaten by some laypeople, such as His fasting, prayers, and the completion of things befitting humanity with His life-giving sufferings. These are the matters that the unbelievers argue about, while the believers burn them with the fire of the Holy Spirit, removing their form from their hearts, knowing that He is the incarnate God who is completely both natures united together in one.

It is said that nothing of it shall remain until morning, meaning to illuminate this present life in the evening, and the morning is the coming age, so that we do not neglect anything we have been commanded and do not keep any doubt in His command, lest we demand it if we find something of it in that future age after death.

It is said that none of its bones shall be broken, as mentioned by John the Evangelist when the soldiers came and broke the legs of the thieves who were crucified with Him.

When they came to Jesus and found that he was already dead, they did not break His legs. Instead, one of the soldiers pierced Jesus' side with a spear, bringing a sudden flow of blood and water. This fulfilled the scripture that says, "Not one of his bones will be broken" (John 19:33-36, Psalm 34:20). This passage refers to the Passover lamb. The evangelist understood that all of this was a prophecy about the Lord Christ, and he wrote it to teach us about the perfection of grace, first and foremost. As it is written in the Law, "Do this in remembrance of your deliverance from the bondage of the Egyptians."

The Lord said, "This is a new covenant. I have made a new agreement with you, so do this in remembrance of me." I have made a covenant with you for salvation, and I have renewed you after the affliction. By this new covenant, the old Passover is abolished, as it was not the ultimate goal but rather a preserved example until perfection. As the apostle said, "All that was in the Law was only a shadow of what was to come, not the reality itself but a symbol of it." The Lord commanded us to do this in remembrance of Him, specifically the Passover of salvation, always in the manner in which we saw the High Priest, the Lord Christ, and not as a memorial of a prophet or messenger, but as a perpetual memorial to the Lord, to whom be glory forever. He commanded us to do this until his coming. Just as in the act of the Passover, the Lord destroyed the firstborn of the Egyptians with the final blow. Similarly, in the act of this Passover, that is, offering himself on the cross, the Lord destroyed the leaders of the rebellious demons who enslaved humanity in earthly works. He did not allow them to seek what is fitting for the heavens. When Jesus declared himself on the cross, crying out, "Father, into your hands I commit my spirit," He revealed that the one suffering for us is the Son of God. Then He revealed in Hades that His Spirit is united with the glory of His divinity, and He judged the enemy with justice, stripping him of his power and weapon that the nations had relied on, and had served as a god. He humiliated their greatness and cast it into hell!

Just as when the Lord destroyed the firstborn of the Egyptians, the rest were afraid, saying, "We will all perish." Likewise, when the Lord destroyed the leader of the demons, whom Isaiah spoke of as "How you have fallen from heaven, O morning star, son of the dawn" (Isaiah 14:12), the soldiers were afraid, and they were exposed. They learned that they too would perish. As the apostle testified, he nullified the document of our sins that stood against us and took it away, nailing it to His cross. By openly revealing His hypostasis, He shamed the demons, their leaders, and their rulers.

As the Lord commanded Moses to strike the sea with the staff in his hand, the sea split apart, and the children of Israel crossed through it while Pharaoh and his soldiers drowned in it. This was the perfect salvation of the people from the slavery of

Pharaoh. In the same way, the Lord descended into hell with his soul united with divinity, and the sign of the cross before Him shattered the gates of bronze, broke the iron bars, and brought out the souls trapped there since Adam, crossing them through the depths of the sea, the abyss, the utmost darkness, trampling death and hell with the power of His divinity. His soul did not remain in hell, as written, nor did His body see corruption. For He was united with his life-giving divinity and did not separate from His humanity, leading the souls to the true promised land, the holy place that He inherited with His right hand.

Pharaoh, who is the devil, drowned in the depths of the sea of fire, which is the ultimate salvation for the believing people. He prepared it for the devil's army after him for eternity. Just as Moses lifted up the serpent in the wilderness, so must the Son of Man be lifted up so that everyone who believes in Him may not perish but have eternal life. Just as the bronze serpent did not contain the venom of death and only healed those who looked at it from the deadly venom, Christ united with a complete human body like ours, sin alone excepted, through which sin is removed and we are saved from it when we look at Him with the eye of faith. Just as Moses, by stretching out His hands, defeated Joshua son of Nun and the Israelites against the giants who fought and hindered them from entering the promised land. When Moses raised his hands, the Israelites prevailed, and when he lowered them, the giants prevailed. When Moses' hands grew weary, they placed stones for him to sit on, and Aaron and Hur held up his hands, one from one side and the other from the other. Moses' hands remained steady until sunset, and Joshua defeated the giants and killed many of them with the edge of the sword. God said to Moses, "I will utterly blot out the memory of Amalek from under heaven." Similarly, when our race fought against Amalek, who is the devil, and his enemies of truth to hinder us from entering the true promised land, namely the eternal kingdom prepared by God for all His saints.

The Lord came for our salvation, and since He is not incarnate and does not appear, he united with a human body to accept pain on our behalf.

And so He was lifted up on the cross, and He stretched out His holy hands with the power of divinity, conquering the devil, and He remained with His hands outstretched until sunset. And it was written that this is how God will destroy the enemies from under the heavens, meaning the enemy who fights against the human race, so that they may not enter into the eternal rest that God promised to all the righteous. And just as Moses' hands were supported by two, Aaron and Hur, so the Lord's cross was completed with two, the building of Israel and the nations. And just as Moses sat on the stones with his hands outstretched until the end of the day, so the Lord made his name on the holy church built on the rock of faith forever! This is the church that He purchased with His precious blood on the holy cross.

These things and others like them were done by Moses and were a prophecy of the Lord Christ, as the Lord said to the Jews. That was written for My sake. And He testified to his disciples on the road to Emmaus when He began to explain to them what was in the Law and the Prophets and all the books about His sufferings and resurrection, so that we may understand this after them. And we know that it was by His will that he endured these sufferings. And that is why He allowed the prophets to speak by the Spirit. As He wished, He became incarnate because where He was invisible and not suffering in his essence of divinity, He united with the flesh to bear the sufferings for us. Additionally, He did not unite with a soulless mind, but with a speaking, rational soul. This is the one who accepted the sufferings and tasted death, and He declared this saying, "I lay down My life to

V Crucifixion

take it up again, and no one takes it from Me, but I lay it down of My own accord, and I have the authority to lay it down, and I have the authority to take it up again."

Oh the wonder that surpasses all understanding?! The one who could not suffering in His divinity accepted suffering in the flesh for us!! The King of kings and the Lord of all the earth was conspired against by the rulers of the nations, so that what was written in David might be fulfilled, saying: "Why do the nations rage and the peoples plot in vain, the kings of the earth set themselves, and the rulers take counsel together against the Lord and against his Anointed."

The one who spoke in the Law, the Prophets, the Apostles, and who gave speech to humans was silent in judgment, so that what was written in Isaiah might be fulfilled, saying, "Like a lamb that is led to the slaughter, and like a sheep before its shearers is silent."

He who is feared by all the kings and rules over all the kingdoms. Because of his humility, Herod and his servants despised him, so that what was written in Isaiah might be fulfilled, saying, "He had no form or majesty that we should look at Him, and no beauty that we should desire Him. He was despised and rejected by men, a man of sorrows and acquainted with grief... But He was wounded for our transgressions, crushed for our iniquities; upon Him was the chastisement that brought us peace, and with His stripes we are healed" (Isaiah 53).

The one wrapped in light is like one wearing a red robe. As written in Isaiah: "Who is this coming from Edom, from Bozrah, with his garments stained crimson? Who is this, robed in splendour, striding forward in the greatness of His strength?" The prophet had seen in the spirit the sufferings of the Messiah and marvelled, saying: "Who is this coming from Edom?" For Edom symbolizes heaven, as David said, "Who will lead me to the fortified city? Who will guide me to Edom?" This is where the Lord came from for our salvation, as it is said, "His garments are red, like those of one treading the winepress." Bozrah is interpreted as the place of judgment. The Lord came forth wearing red and purple robes. The Lord answered him at that time in the spirit, saying: "I speak in righteousness, mighty to save." This means that He alone is righteous, and for the sake of our great salvation, He came. The prophet, astonished, asked:

"Why is your apparel red, and your garments like one who treads the winepress?" (Isaiah 63) The Lord also answered him, saying: "I have trodden the winepress alone; from the nations no one was with Me. I trampled them in My anger and trod them down in my Wrath." This is similar to when the Lord said to His disciples: "You will leave me all alone. Yet I am not alone, for my Father is with me." And when He said, "I trampled them in My wrath," it signifies that He is the ruling avenger, and He shed their blood on the ground, meaning their souls descended to the depths of the earth, that is, hell.

He said that the day of retribution has come upon them, meaning the impending judgment. He said, "The year of redemption has come," meaning that every year they performed the Passover ritual, but there was no redemption or fulfilment in it, only a foreshadowing of what was to come. But this particular year, redemption came with the perfect Passover, the Lamb without blemish, meaning the Messiah. He said, "I looked, but there was no one to help, I was appalled that no one gave support; so My own arm achieved salvation for Me," meaning that all were nothing. When I saw their agreement in evil, My strong arm, My invincible divinity, saved Me!

Today, my beloved, the shepherd of shepherds will go like a lamb to the slaughter, fulfilling the prophecy of the prophet Isaiah.

V Crucifixion

He who surpasses all sufferings endured in the flesh for us, to save us from the necessary pains upon us, and deliver us from the judgment of death, as previously stated by the prophet Isaiah, "By His wounds we are healed."

He who is the source of life flows for us, and quenches every thirst, give him vinegar on a stick of the cross to drink. As written in the psalm, "When I was thirsty, they gave me vinegar to drink!" He who bestows crowns of glory and honour on the martyrs, crowned with a crown of thorns, who grants the crown of glory to humans in His eternal kingdom.

He who adorned the sky with clouds and beautified the earth with flowers, they cast lots for His garment to fulfil what was written in David's saying: "They divided my garments among them and cast lots for my clothing."

The sun darkened for the sake of the Sun of righteousness to fulfil what was written in the prophet Amos. On that day, the Lord says the sun will set at noon and the earth will be darkened in broad daylight, the elements will change, the appointed time of the Lord of glory. Because of the wood of the cross.

The earth shook!! The forces of heaven trembled!! The rocks split!! And the tombs opened!! And the dead rose!!

As for the chief priests, they persisted in their error and led the people astray as written about them in the prophet Isaiah saying: "My people, your leaders mislead you and confuse the course of your paths," (Isaiah 3) to fulfil the word of the Lord upon them that they did not enter and did not allow those who were entering to enter.

And when they witnessed the disturbance oN the face of heaven and earth, they were not afraid, to the extent that the rocks melted but their hearts did not soften. And out of their intense envy, they did not reflect on that but were eager to kill

Him so that His name would not be exalted over them. As for the thief on the right, even though he was a reckless killer, he pondered what had happened and realized it within himself, saying in truth, "This is the Christ the Lord." And for His sake, all this happened. He did not hesitate or turn away from the pain of crucifixion and death, but He cried out loudly saying, "Remember me, O Lord, when you come into your kingdom."

Look at his good faith and how he first began to blame himself when his companion rebuked him to be silent, saying:

Truly, we are being punished justly, for we are getting what our deeds deserve. But this man has done nothing wrong … Then he cried out to him with a sincere confession filled with faith, saying: "Remember me, Lord, when you come into your kingdom."

Let the scribes of the Jews now be ashamed, who read the Law. They are teachers to others. For they only read the ink and accept the paper, but they do not understand the Spirit that is in the book.

And because of their evil and wickedness, there was no spirit of God in them. For the spirit of the prophets is subject to the prophets as it is written. Truly, they are like a fig tree. Which only had leaves. They resemble the leaves of the Law that they read, and there was no fruit in them, which is the work of the Law, because it points to the Christ, and for this reason they were cursed and they no longer bear fruit forever.

Because priesthood, prophecy, and kingship have ceased among them, along with the rest of the work of the first law, as its goal is the Messiah, and they have been scattered among all nations. They will be humiliated and disgraced when they hear that a thief is reading the books. When he saw what had suddenly happened, he demonstrated the work of the law with his

V Crucifixion

righteous certainty and cried out declaring, "Remember me, O Lord, when you come into your kingdom."

And because the Lord, out of His compassion, did not leave them without showing wonders at the time of their stubbornness, but rather various wonders He brought forth suddenly in the heavens and on earth, in order to attract their minds. When they persisted in their wickedness, the argument was against them. Then permission was granted to the thief to contemplate this and cry out in the midst of the crowd, weeping for them, displaying the greatness of His divinity, saying, "Remember me, O Lord, when you come into your kingdom."

Now look at the power of this word!! He asked to be remembered while knowing that He was not a human, but rather acknowledged and confessed that He is the Lord of glory!! And at what time will He be remembered? He said at his coming in His second manifestation in the glory of His kingdom. Indeed, when he witnessed these signs with true discernment, the Lord increased his radiance until he achieved a good understanding, because to him who has, more will be given. He did not only forewarn of his first coming, but also of the future one, which will be in His glorious and fearsome majesty with His holy forces. And out of fervent faith, he did not fear this but cried out saying, "Remember me, O Lord, when you come into your kingdom."

It is truly astonishing that the disciples were in hiding, and the sick who had been healed by the Lord of all kinds of ailments did not acknowledge Him at that time, but rather the thief cried out in the midst of that celebratory crowd like a heralding charioteer, saying, "Remember me, O Lord, when you come into your kingdom!"

And the Lord, full of mercy and compassion, gave him more than he asked and wished for, and answered him with a voice filled with comfort, saying, "Truly, I say to you, today you will be with Me in paradise!"

Today, my beloved, Christ presented himself as a lamb. He offered a sacrifice for our sins, as written about Him, the great high priest as the apostle called Him. For this special day, He offered himself as a sacrifice, saying: He offered himself once to abolish sin, as the true God who to Him is offered sacrifices. He accepted requests and forgave sins, saying to the thief: "Truly I tell you, today you will be with me in paradise", for the Holy Trinity is truly one in divinity. He is all three: He is the sacrifice, the priest who offers the sacrifice for sins, and the God who forgives sins. As the apostle told us about these things, saying: "Christ offered himself once. And by His resurrection, He washed away many sins." Therefore, when he offered himself as a sacrifice on the cross like the high priest, He revealed the work of divinity, and told the thief: "Truly I tell you, today you will be with Me in paradise." The Lord completed these three on the wood of the cross. The thief humbly asked to be remembered in His kingdom. He was granted entry into paradise before anyone else. It is truly amazing that all the prophets and righteous people from Adam to the coming of Christ awaited this day, carrying the burden of the day and enduring its length, yet this thief deserved to enter paradise before them!

This is because he was present with the Lord the King. The Lord said to him truthfully, saying as one who swears by his right hand: Today you are present here, and for many future ages you will be with Me, exclusively and no one else, in the paradise of bliss!

When the thief surrendered his spirit, the divine Pantocrator, present everywhere, seized him and brought him to the eternal paradise!

V Crucifixion

Do you not see that all the kings of the earth, who are human like us, have their authority valid in all corners of their kingdom? How much more powerful is the kingdom that rules over all, controls the heavens and the earth and everything in it simply by the divine authority, doing as it pleases and executing its command without hindrance, as all are subject to the sovereignty of its lordship.

Blessed are you, O thief, who in one hour became righteous and a friend. For you were blessed by the Lord with entry into paradise before your father Adam and those with him from long ago. Let those who condemn their brothers be ashamed now, for their outward appearance in their present time, as they do not know what awaits us and them in the hereafter! And how the meeting with the Lord will be after death. Let them look at Judas, who was counted among the disciples, and at the thief who was numbered among the killers!

And how in one night and one day both changed, Judas fell from the glory of discipleship and strangled himself and went to eternal damnation, while the thief entered paradise before all the righteous and obtained an eternal life that never ends!!

And when our Lord Jesus Christ accepted all these pains on the cross for us, my beloved ones. He knew that the time had come for Him to surrender His spirit. And to save the imprisoned souls, He handed over His blessed mother Mary to His disciple John the Evangelist, because he alone stood by his cross without the rest of the disciples, as the high priest knew him. So Saint John took her to his house so that she would not see Him when He handed over His spirit and be troubled, for the Lord is a compassionate God in all things!!

After all this, when He knew that everything was completed, to fulfil what was written, He said, "I am thirsty," thirsty for the spring of life to quench us from his inexhaustible fullness!! He was the One who had said "he who is thirsty, let him come to Me and drink" and He said to the Samaritan woman, "Whoever drinks the water that I give him will never thirst again. Because the water I give in it is a spring of eternal life." Yet one of the soldiers took a sponge, filled it with vinegar, and put it on a hyssop branch and brought it to His mouth. When He had drunk the vinegar, He said, "It is finished."

The scripture says, "They gave me vinegar to drink when I was thirsty." He said, "I am thirsty" not because vinegar quenches thirst, but to fulfil what was written.

Also, the wicked Jews' plot is revealed. And all they did was against the law they claim to adhere to, because it was customary to give water to those they wanted to kill. But when Jesus asked for water, they gave him vinegar. The scripture says, "He bowed His head and gave up His spirit." Meaning, He died by choice, not by force. Matthew and Mark mentioned the cry He made in Hebrew, which is the beginning of Psalm 22, "My God, my God, why have you forsaken me." This was to draw the minds of the understanding to the rest of the psalm, where David recounts the rest of the Lord's pains, their gathering against Him, their mocking Him, the nails, the dividing of His garments by lot, saying, "Dogs have surrounded me, a band of evil men has encircled me. They have pierced My hands and My feet. They divide My garments among them and cast lots for My clothing. They say, 'Let Him be delivered, let Him be saved, if He delights in Him.' That is why the Lord mentioned the beginning of this psalm on the cross. He did not mention it in any other language except Hebrew, in which it was written, so that they would understand when they read it!!

Matthew and Mark also mentioned the gall, and that the Lord cried out with a loud voice and surrendered His spirit so that we may know that He surrendered His spirit by of His own will,

V Crucifixion

not by weakness. As for Luke, he clarifies the voice for us, saying that Jesus cried out with a loud voice, saying, "Father, into Your hands I commit My spirit." And when He said this, He surrendered His spirit. It is known that one who weakens and becomes mute surrenders His spirit with effort. As for Christ, He cried out with a loud voice to declare that He is the Son of God. He said, "I lay down my life to take it up again. I have the power to lay it down, and I have the power to take it up again, and no one can take it from Me."

He said, "Here, Father, I commit My spirit into your hands," because it is the hand of the Father and His power, as the Apostle said, and that the Holy Trinity are of one will.

He said this when surrendering His spirit, because Satan had dominion over souls since Adam due to disobedience. So when the Lord came from heaven, incarnated and became the second Adam for the hope of renewed life, He said, "Father," to declare that He is the only Son of God. He said, "Into your hands," referring to the one who is one with Him in divinity.

He said, "I commit My spirit," meaning just as Satan had dominion over souls through Adam, so through me, from now on, they will be saved and be in your hands, O Mighty One. And the Apostle says, just as in Adam all die, so in Christ all will be made alive.

The Holy Gospel says, at the moment of the cry, the veil of the temple was torn in two from top to bottom. This means that the Holy Spirit, who was active in the old law, was removed from it, as its purpose was for the coming of Christ.

When the spirit was removed from the temple of the Jews, the veil of the temple was torn at that moment, because the sacrifices of animals and the blood of goats ceased by His offering for all and the fulfilment of the goal.

He said, "The earth shook, the rocks split, and the tombs were opened, and many bodies of the saints who had fallen asleep were raised. After His resurrection, they came out of their tombs and entered the holy city and appeared to many, fulfilling the prophecy."

The soul descended to Hades united with divinity, saving souls, and the body on the cross united with divinity, raised bodies!! As for the earthquake, it proclaims His power and that His death was not due to weakness over death!! His death, which shook the earth by declaring the power of His voice. And that His death was by His will and His desire!! He who said, "I have the power to lay down My life and I have the power to take it up."

As for the splitting of the rocks, let those whose hearts are as hard as their flesh weep, as they claim!! How could the solid rocks split, while those who read the law did not soften their hearts and did not repent to be forgiven by His abundant mercy.

The Gospel said: "As for the centurion and those with him who were guarding Jesus, when they saw the earthquake and what had happened, they were very afraid and said, 'Truly this was the Son of God!' I mean the Gentiles who did not have the law, including the centurion and the soldiers with him. When they saw the signs that occurred during the earthquake at the moment of the spirit's surrender, they were very afraid and their hearts were humbled. By observing the creations, they inferred about the Creator and said, 'Truly this was the Son of God!' They did not read a book, but they heard from the Jews when they complained to Pilate saying, 'He claimed to be the Son of God.' Therefore, when they saw it, they said "this statement was true, that He was indeed the Son of God in truth without doubt or falsehood." The scripture said: "And all the crowd that had gathered, upon witnessing this scene, returned while beating their chests!" I mean when they saw the occurring signs, they

V Crucifixion

could not bear to stay, but they returned regretfully for what the wicked chief priests had done, and they were striking their chests out of sorrow and pain!

When all these terrifying things were completed, then the Lord commanded the sun to return to its usual brightness at its setting after nine hours of daylight, and nature calmed down and settled, to declare that He was pleased with the earth and those on it. That His crucifixion was for mercy, not for vengeance and anger, but He made these signs to show His power. And He restored the light of the sun to fulfil what was written in the prophecy of Zechariah, saying: 'It will be one day known to the Lord. It will not be day or night. But at evening time there will be light.' Now look at the prophet's statement that it will be one day. I mean that there will be no other. As the apostle said: 'He offered Himself once.'

The Prophet said: "And that day is known to the Lord." I mean that it is special and known forever to commemorate His sufferings. He said there is no day or night, meaning it is divided and has the light of day and the darkness of night. Then he said, "And there will be light in the evening." This prophecy clearly indicates that the sunlight will be close to evening as it happened!! Then after that, the Jews who did not have their hearts humbled went to Pilate and asked him to break the legs of the crucified so they would die quickly and be taken down for the sake of the Sabbath night. Because that Sabbath was important to them as it was the Sabbath of the seven days of unleavened bread. Then the soldiers came as messengers from Pilate, these are different from the first soldiers who believed and broke the legs of the thieves who were crucified with Him. When they came to the One who knows all things before their time, they found that He had already given up His spirit willingly so they did not break His legs, fulfilling the Scripture that says no bone shall be broken!! I mean the statement that was made earlier about the

Passover lamb, which is a symbol of Christ. But one of those wicked soldiers who came with them wanted to test Him, so he stabbed Him in the side with a spear to fulfil what was written by the Prophet Zechariah: "They will look on the one they have pierced", and for a time water and blood came out!!

The water signifies that He died in truth, surrendering His soul. And the blood also signifies that He is alive in truth by the unity of the divinity with His living body without separation. Because each of them was separate, I mean the water and the blood without mixing.

And here the Prophet David declares this matter clearly in Psalm 69, saying: "They gave me vinegar to drink." I mean the vinegar mixed with gall that they gave Him when they wanted to crucify Him.

He tasted it and did not want to drink it, as the prophet witnessed. He also said: "When I was thirsty, they gave me vinegar to drink." I mean their action was an act of healing with contempt outside the law of the Torah, and also outside the law of the kings which was customary. But what did He say after that? He said, "Let their table become a snare and a trap, a stumbling block and a retribution for them." By their table I mean their service, which was the sacrifices of animals that were a symbol of the precious body and blood of the Lord. It is through His blood especially that He cleanses all. So when the truth came and they did not accept it, that which was useless to them became a stumbling block and a sure offense to them, because they clung to the shadow and abandoned the truth.

He said: "Their eyes were darkened so that they could not see." I mean they were blinded to the knowledge of the light of truth coming into the world. As the Lord compared them to blind men leading the blind, and He also said to them, "The light is

V Crucifixion

with you for a little while longer. Walk while you have the light, lest darkness overtake you."

He said, "And their appearance will always be curved from time to time, meaning under the strange kings who ruled over them, like the captivity of Babylon.

He said, "Pour out your wrath upon them. Let your fierce anger overtake them." I mean the captivity of Vespasian for them, with the severe killing that they suffered from him. This happened quickly after the Lord's ascension by forty years.

He said, "Let their dwellings be made desolate." I mean their desolation by destroying them with the sword, along with the exile and dispersion that befell the rest as you see now.

He said, "And let no one dwell in their homes to rebuild them." I mean the desolation of Jerusalem and the temple, and the cessation of services in it.

He said, "Because they persecuted the one who was afflicted." I mean that He came humbly and accepted the things that were necessary for us to be saved, as the apostle said: "since He was tempted and suffered, he is able to help those who are tempted and suffering." But instead of accepting him, they persecuted him. He said, "And they added wounds to the wounded!!" I mean they stabbed him with a spear, which they added after nailing the nails, because this was done without the authority of kings or the justice of the public, as the stab was after the surrender of the spirit!! This was foolishness and hatred from them. That is why the prophet David mentioned these two actions specifically in this matter, betrayal and stabbing. And he first called for their destruction in this world, as happened to them. Then hereafter he called for their eternal destruction forever. He said, "Increase their sins because they have sinned. I mean the sin they committed against the prophets, so they will increase their sins many times over for what they did to the Lord of the prophets. As the Lord said, all this will come upon this generation and they will be punished for it. For the blood of all the righteous that was shed on earth, from the blood of Abel to the blood of Zechariah. This is because they abandoned the coming of the Messiah.

He said, "And they will not enter into your justice." I mean his justice of equality for all in the faith, so they do not deserve it because they did not obey.

He said, "They will be erased from the book of life." I mean the book of life mentioned by Moses and the prophets, they will be erased from it.

He said, "And they will not be written with your righteous ones." I mean those who are justified by grace freely through our Lord Jesus Christ. They will not have a share in that, nor a portion for their disbelief and arrogance.

These prophecies and their like, my beloved, the Lord fulfilled on the wood of the holy cross for us. To bring us the life worthy of Him. He who is without pain was pleased to suffer pain in the flesh for us, to bring us healing from pain. He who is above all and surpasses all glory and honour, was pleased to suffer for us, to bring us to the glory worthy of Him. The giver of life was pleased to become flesh for us to bring us to the life suitable for His eternal greatness.

O Christ, who suffered for us, we worship You, and we bow down to Your pains and crucifixion.

We glorify Your pains and magnify Your holy cross. We acknowledge Your suffering and proclaim Your resurrection.

We await Your coming, where you will judge us, for through this we have righteousness, purification, salvation, and glory. We sing with the apostle who said, "But far be it from me to boast

V Crucifixion

except in the cross of our Lord Jesus Christ, by which the world has been crucified to me, and I to the world." This is the same cross that the holy angels boasted about, saying to the women, "You seek Jesus who was crucified. He is not here, for He has risen." And in the place where the Lord was, they confessed the crucified one as the Lord of glory, and they glorified and proclaimed to the women about it.

We must give glory and honour to the Lord who chose to suffer for us without any merit on our part, as the apostle preached, saying: "For while we were still weak, at the right time Christ died for the ungodly. For one will scarcely die for a righteous person—though perhaps for a good person one would dare even to die."

From here we know God's love for us, that while we were sinners, Christ died for us.

He also said, "You who once were alienated and hostile in mind, doing evil deeds, He has now reconciled in His body of flesh by His death, in order to present you holy and blameless and above reproach before Him." Let us not forget now His life-giving pains, as he instructed us to remember them every time during the offering of the holy mysteries, until His coming in the glory of his kingdom. And we sing, saying, "O Christ the Lord, we worship you, and we bow down to your beloved pains and your crucifixion. We look at you with the eye of faith and survive the venom of the old serpent, which deceived our father Adam and expelled him from paradise, and he and his descendants were not healed except by the Lord being lifted on the cross. He, being eternal, gives life to all who look at Him with the eye of faith, not for temporal life, but for eternal life as is fitting." The apostle commands us to strive now with patience in the struggle that is set before us, and to look to Jesus, who became the pioneer and perfector of our faith, who for the joy that was set before him endured the cross, despising the shame. Then he affirmed, saying, "Consider Him who endured from sinners such hostility against Himself, so that you may not grow weary or fainthearted." He commanded us to keep the pains of Christ in our thoughts, written on our hearts, engraved on our hands, pictured before our eyes, standing before us.

By the power of the Cross we are saved, for by the Cross the righteous were saved, those who were and those who will be. By the Cross the salvation of the early fathers, the prophets, and all the righteous was accomplished. By the Cross the Lord captivated hell and opened paradise. By the Cross the churches are sanctified. By the Cross the descent of the Holy Spirit upon baptism is completed and we are born as children for the inheritance of eternal life. By the Cross the sanctification of the spiritual mysteries is fulfilled. By the Cross the priesthood is established. By the Cross all the services of apostolic Christianity are completed.

By the Cross the apostles performed miracles. By the Cross the saints worked wonders. By the Cross the saints expelled evil spirits. By the Cross everything is sanctified, for it is the sign of Christ the King. Wherever the sign of the cross is made in sanctifications, the Spirit descends and the sanctification is fulfilled. For the Cross is the sign of the Son, and the Spirit acts in conjunction with that.

The Cross is the light of the Church and is always above the altar. By the Cross the righteous kings boasted, by the Cross Constantine the King and his mother Helena and his sons Constantius and Constans boasted. With the sign of the Cross, Constantine defeated the barbarian armies and the Cross appeared in his days, thus establishing an eternal memory for him. He placed the sign of the Cross above his head on his crown to have power, assistance, and salvation. All believing

V Crucifixion

kings placed the Cross above the crowns on their heads, boasting with it, displaying the splendour of the glory of faith in Christ the true King. Let us also draw the sign of the holy Cross on our faces, and fortify all our bodies with it as we place its mark on all our members.

This sacred example, which first appeared, symbolizes the prophecy when God said to Moses, "Take the rod in your hand, which turned into a serpent, perform wonders with it in Egypt, and strike the Red Sea with it lengthwise and widthwise." The example of the Cross splits!! And this was an example of the holy Cross. The wonders, powers, and sanctifications were not done in one time like what Moses did, but in every time and place. This example was also shown by Jacob Israel when he blessed the sons of Joseph at his death, placing his hands in the form of the Cross and blessing them, then bowing on the head of his staff, showing the example of the Cross from which blessings come, and his bowing on the head of the staff is a sign of the Cross. Just as he placed his right hand on Ephraim's head, the younger, and his left hand on Manasseh's head, the older, and said that Ephraim would receive more than Manasseh, so too the peoples of the nations will be exalted more than the children of Israel, for the Lord's crucifixion was for the nations and the children of Israel together.

We must learn the dignity of the Holy Cross and preserve it with all reverence, as the Lord commanded us to bear the Cross and follow it so that we may deserve it. We must endure the pains of the world, as the Apostle said, that the life of the living is not for themselves but for the one who died for them and rose again to be the Lord of the living and the dead. Let our conduct be fitting to the death of the Lord, for the one who died has been saved from sin and liberated from it, as the Apostle says. He teaches us what death is, saying, "Put to death, therefore, whatever belongs to your earthly nature: sexual immorality, impurity, lust, evil desires, and greed, which is idolatry." He then exhorts us, saying that we should always carry in our bodies the death of Jesus, so that the life of Jesus may also be revealed in our mortal bodies (2 Corinthians 4:10). Therefore, if we, the living, surrender to death for Jesus' sake, and the life of Jesus is revealed in our mortal bodies, it is right for us to resemble the death of the Lord, dying to sin and worldly desires. This is also evident when he says, "In your struggle against sin, you have not yet resisted to the point of shedding your blood" (Hebrews 12:4), and he commands us to depart from the ways of this world in order to inherit the eternal kingdom, saying, "The animals whose blood is brought into the sanctuary by the high priest as a sin offering are burned outside the camp. Therefore Jesus also suffered outside the city gate to make the people holy through his own blood. Let us, then, go to him outside the camp, bearing the disgrace he bore, for here we do not have an enduring city, but we are looking for the city that is to come" (Hebrews 13:11-14).

Look now at the similarity in the Old Testament, how the Lord completed the purification through His precious blood, and did not require us to shed blood due to the weakness of humanity, but commanded us to depart from the ways of the world, bearing the sign of the Cross by which we are distinguished from unbelievers. It is to us glory and salvation! And He teaches us that we do not remain eternal in this world, so our hope must be in the promised kingdom that is everlasting.

Let us love our brothers for the one who loved us and gave himself for us, and let us have mercy on the poor for the one who had mercy on the captives and the lost and died for all. Let us make peace and reconciliation with our sisters for the one who reconciled all people through the blood of His Cross, uniting all who were far. Let us keep our bodies and all our senses pure so that we may die with Christ to the ways of this world, and let us

V Crucifixion

visit the imprisoned for the one who brought out the captives because of Adam and brought them into paradise.

This is the behaviour to follow, and perseverance in keeping His commandments.

And we ask the one who humbled Himself among the hypocrites for our sake, and suffered for our comfort, and died for our lives, to guard us all and have mercy on us with the abundance of His mercy, along with those whom He has made a covenant with them for salvation through His holy cross, and inspire us to follow His commandments and grant us rest and forgiveness in His dreadful judgment. Through the intercession of our blessed, pure, and immaculate Lady Mary, the honourable and pure apostles, the martyrs and the righteous saints, and those whom the Lord is pleased with their good deeds. Amen.

VI

Holy Resurrection

Translated from the arabic edition
by Fr Mancarius Awad

In the name of the Father, and of the Son, and of the Holy Spirit, one God, Amen.

The glorious Resurrection.

By the honourable Abba Bulus al-Bushi

May his prayers and blessings cover us until the last breath, Amen.

O You who rose from among the dead, trampled death, and bestowed upon us a new life that is not in affliction.

O our Christ, awaken our dead minds so that we may behold the glory of Your incomprehensible divinity.

O Holy Lord, who abolished the pains of death through His holy resurrection, abolish from us the forces of the deadly enemy of the soul, so that we may walk with You in everlasting life.

O Eternal Master, establish in us the hope of the coming eternal life that has no end, and plant in our hearts the hope of the blessings of Your eternal kingdom.

O Merciful and Compassionate One, who through His holy resurrection granted our kind the authority to have a share with Him in the promised resurrection.

Grant us also a portion in that inheritance with all Your saints, O Good One, the overseer of all things.

O You who transformed our weak body to be like the body of Your glory in an imperishable blissful life, grant us strength here to move from routine habits to glorious virtuous deeds, so that we may deserve a noble transition with all Your saints who pleased You from the beginning. Grant me also, O Lord - You who freely gave life through Your holy resurrection to all creation - the ability to speak of Your resurrection from the dead.

VI Holy Resurrection

Grant me understanding, O Leader of Life, who gave His life through His resurrection for all the perishing, so that I may speak of the deed of Your invincible power.

Grant me speech, O Emmanuel our God, who granted the world redemption from death through His promised resurrection, so that I may speak of the strength of Your might and the beauty of the light of Your resurrection that illuminated the entire universe.

Now I begin and say:

Christ is risen from the dead, He who died trampled death, and to those in the tombs He granted eternal life.

He who died abolished the sting of death. He who descended with the power of His divinity to Hades, took captivity captive, and saved the souls that awaited Him. He opened the gate of paradise with the hope of life for all nations who had no hope. He prepared for us the way to the kingdom. He repaired for us a path leading to the new life. He opened before us a door leading to eternal dwellings.

How can the born of the earth treasure eternal life if the ruler of Life and the Lord of Hosts did not unite with them and grant them a life befitting of Him?! How can the prisoner be justified if the incarnate God does not unite with their weak humanity and convey to them the glory befitting Him?! How can the one who perishes put on the imperishable if the Lord God, who does not change or fade away, does not incarnate from their humanity?!

So He granted them incorruption. And the ruler of life became the first to rise from among the dead. And just as death came to a human of dust, so did life come from the righteous heavenly Lord alone. He who is without sin and has the power to forgive sins. He alone is righteous without fault, and has the ability to justify and give life eternally as is fitting.

Just as the death that came to us from our father Adam was not strange to us, but came to us in relation to our humanity to him. Likewise, the life that came to us through Christ was not strange to us. Rather, it came to us in relation to His incarnation from us as a favour from Him to us.

So our death was just, but life was given by grace and mercy!!

Truly, we boast in the Lord as it is written and exalt in God our Saviour and rejoice in His salvation.

And just as God created the wilderness from the beginning as a favour from Him to it and not out of need for it. Likewise, it was the duty of His justice to form a covenant with His creation. Not out of need for it, but as a favour from Him and mercy. He first created it with temporal life, and then made a covenant with it again and renewed it with eternal life!!

Firstly: He made it for the world of perishing, and the place of toil and affliction.

Secondly: He raised it to the world of eternity, and the place of comfort, bliss, and joy.

And when our father Adam was created and placed in the paradise of bliss, He commanded him saying: "Of all the trees you may eat, except for this one tree you shall not eat from. For on the day you eat from it, you shall surely die."

So Adam ate and did not die on that day. Rather, he died after nine hundred and thirty years.

And the word of God does not become void, but just as the tangible death is the separation of the soul from the body, so the rational death is the separation of God's spirit from man. Because with the separation of the superior from the inferior, the death of the inferior is undoubted, because it is the cause of its life. Since Adam ate from the tree of disobedience, God's spirit was taken away from him, so he died a rational death, which is the true death. Because the tangible death is nothing but a transition for those who follow God's commandments. So when God took His Holy Spirit from Adam on that day when he ate from the forbidden tree, he died a rational death, and then He judged him with the tangible death, saying: "Cursed is the ground because of you. Thorns and thistles it shall bring forth for you. By the sweat of your face you shall eat bread till you return to the ground, for out of it you were taken; for dust you are, and to dust you shall return."

So God executed the rational death in him on that day, and then judged him with the tangible death. Thus, he lost the hope of both lives, as well as his descendants after him. None of his descendants were able to restore to us the eternal life that is without end, because it is not suitable for them. Because the life that is without end is only for the One who is endless. And this was none other than God. But He does not bring us to it with His divinity, because we cannot bear that. So, He graciously brought us to it through the miraculous incarnation!

Because where His divinity is not seen, He united with a complete human body like us in everything except sin alone. He brought life to that united body. Then He accepted suffering for us. He showed Himself victorious over suffering and death by His resurrection from the dead. Then He brought us eternal life in relation to that body taken from us.

And this was an additional grace, because He wanted us not to be estranged from Him. He included us in that second birth and the acceptance of the Holy Spirit. And He gave us of His life-giving mysteries as He said, "Unless you eat the flesh of the Son of Man and drink His blood, you have no life in you.

Whoever eats My flesh and drinks My blood abides in Me, and I in him" (John 6:53).

Without this mystery, no one can inherit the kingdom of heaven. And even though the Lord raised the dead to show His power, they also died a second time and returned to their dust, awaiting the general resurrection of all. But the Lord, being the firstborn of the resurrection from the dead, does not die again as the apostle said. Thus, He became the first in the resurrection and the leader of all blessings.

And when humans saw the body that was once dead rise from the dead, alive and incorruptible by the power of divinity, they knew that vengeance had passed, death had ended, life had come, and salvation had arrived. This was not by a human, but by the power of the Lord God of hosts.

Let us recite today with the Apostle Paul saying:

"But now Christ is risen from the dead, the first fruits of those who have fallen asleep. For since by man came death, by man also came the resurrection of the dead. For as in Adam all die, so also in Christ all will be made alive. But each in his own order: Christ the first fruits, after that those who are Christ's at His coming, then comes the end" (1 Corinthians 15:20-24).

And in another letter he said: "For if by the transgression of one, death reigned through the one, much more those who receive the abundance of grace and of the gift of righteousness will reign in life through the One, Jesus Christ. So then as through one transgression there resulted condemnation to all men, even so through one act of righteousness there resulted justification of life to all men. For as through the one man's disobedience the many were made sinners, even so through the obedience of the One the many will be made righteous" (Romans 5:17-19).

VI Holy Resurrection

This gift has been fulfilled for us today, my beloved, by the resurrection of our Lord Jesus Christ. Through which our hearts rejoice and find comfort in remembering His glorious sufferings that He endured for us.

Today, my beloved, the words of David have been fulfilled, saying: "Weeping may last for the night, but a shout of joy comes in the morning," because the women who were mourning and weeping for Him yesterday evening, when the morning dawned today, the angels returned from the tomb with great joy to inform His pure and holy apostles that the Lord has risen and is going ahead of you to Galilee!! Then He added to their joy and happiness with what He said to them after the angel's message. They rejoiced and came forward, took hold of His feet, and worshiped Him. Then the compassionate God removed from them the fear that had troubled them from the wicked Jews, by saying to them, "Do not be afraid." I mean, you have seen Me and your hearts have been revived.

Then He said, "Go and tell my brothers to go to Galilee; there they will see me." Oh, what a hope and comfort that knows no bounds.

He called humans His brothers for the sake of the wondrous incarnation. As it is written, "I will proclaim Your name to My brothers." And if they keep His commandments, they will be raised like Him without corruption, for He is the symbol of their life. And the only Son became the firstborn among many brothers, as the Apostle testified. And yet He did not forsake His uniqueness, for He is the only begotten Son of the Father before all ages, and the firstborn among many brothers in the resurrection from the dead.

Now, my beloved, let us praise the resurrection of our Lord Jesus Christ. By which our race was honoured. And He granted us eternal rest here. Let us hasten to the tomb in spirit with Peter and John. And let us hold His feet with the blessed Mary, His mother, and the other Mary, and worship Him and kiss them. Then let us rise walking on the road to Emmaus with Luke and his companion Cleopas, to hear from them the Holy One's interpretations of the books that were spoken by the Spirit about His sufferings and resurrection.

Then let us quickly return with them to the eleven and cry out with one accord with everyone saying truly the Lord has risen. Let us go to Galilee swiftly and without delay. Let us worship with the eleven pure apostles and hear Him saying: "All authority has been given to Me in heaven and on earth" and how He commanded them saying: "Go to all nations and baptize them in the name of the Father and the Son and the Holy Spirit." Let us enter into the closed upper room, and behold the Lord - who has the power to pass through all things without hindrance - giving peace to His creatures, the leaders of all creation, our holy fathers, the pure apostles, the honourable ones. Let us contemplate how He gave them the life-giving Spirit by the breath of life.

This is the one who was taken from our father Adam, the first ancestor, at the time of disobedience. Then He added to them with a better authority to bind and loose. And we cry out to Him with the apostle Thomas saying: "My Lord and my God." Let us hear from Him the known good news and consolation saying: "Blessed are those who have believed and have not seen."

We walk with the apostles, the fishermen, and the people together to the Sea of Galilee and see its wonders after His resurrection, which He showed them there. And how they showed it openly. And we cry out saying: "To You, O Christ our God, we give praise, and by Your life-giving death we proclaim, and by Your holy resurrection we confess. And for Your second coming we wait."

VI Holy Resurrection

Come into our midst today, O David the psalmist, with a ten-stringed harp, so that we may sing with you with joy on this glorious feast.

But we do not say as you said in that time, "Let the Lord arise and His enemies be scattered," because this indicates an intended action that was not completed in your days but by the spirit of prophecy spoke of what was intended. But now this has been fulfilled for us and we rejoice in the salvation. Therefore, we cry out saying the Lord has risen and His enemies have been scattered, those who are the rebellious demons and the unbelieving Jews who He scattered in the corners of the earth and those who oppose Him are destroyed and vanish as smoke vanishes and as wax melts in fire.

Then we hear the Prophet with hopeful eyes saying, "Arise, O Lord, save me, O my God." And he said, "Arise, O my Lord and my God, with the command that I have given." And he said in hope of salvation, "For the sake of the misery of the poor and the sighing of the needy, I arise now. The Lord says: I will make salvation openly" (Psalm 11).

Then he answered with eyes of faith and belief, saying "The words of the Lord are pure words. Like silver refined in a furnace of clay, purified seven times" (Psalm 12) and he spoke of the perfection of the resurrection as if he were seeing it with his own eyes. "The Lord arose like one asleep and like a mighty man who is full of wine and so he drove his enemies back and made them a perpetual disgrace, without covenant," and he said, "Arise, O God, and judge the earth, for you shall inherit all nations." Meaning the entry of nations into faith. Isaiah spoke prophetically on behalf of the people: "You are God and we did not know. The God of Israel and his Saviour."

Behold, the rebellious have been exposed to him and they walk in shame. Zechariah said, "Sing and rejoice, O daughter of

Zion, for behold, I come and will dwell in your midst," says the Lord. And many nations shall flee to the Lord in that day and shall become My people," and here the prophet shows the entry of nations into faith.

The prophet Jeremiah says: "Thus says the Lord, I will quench every thirsty soul, and fill every hungry soul. So I awoke and looked around. Sleep had been sweet to me."

The prophet named the surrender of the Lord's spirit as sleep, because He is alive in divinity, and He is intended to awaken quickly because His body does not see corruption, and David also called it sleep, as he said: "The Lord arose like one asleep," and his saying in Jeremiah: "Sleep had been sweet to me."

As for Solomon, he explained the saying in the Book of Wisdom, saying: "At that time the righteous shall rise up boldly in the face of those who persecuted him and oppressed his efforts, and when they see him they shall be troubled by the intensity of fear."

And they marvel at His wonderful salvation and say among themselves, regretful and remorseful in their souls, thus: We used to mock him in the past and we made him, the one who is new among us, a byword and a disgrace. So how can we now be counted among the children of God and be reckoned among the pure? We have strayed from the path of truth. The light of righteousness did not shine upon us. The sun of truth did not rise upon us. We were immersed in the ways of sin and destruction, and we ran in a wilderness where no one walks. We did not find the way of the Lord. By this I mean the repentance of the people who believed, especially the Jews who were gathered at His crucifixion. As the Apostle Peter wept for them, declaring as it is written in Acts, saying to their leaders:

VI Holy Resurrection

"This is the stone which was rejected by you builders, which has become the chief cornerstone."

Then he said to them all:

"Now all the house of Israel knows that this Jesus, whom you crucified... and by the hands of the leaders you crucified him." Then he urged them about his resurrection from the dead, that his soul was not left in Hades, nor did his flesh see corruption. (Acts 2:22) As it is written about him in the Psalms.

The book says that when they heard this, they were cut to the heart. And about three thousand souls were added to them that day, and after that about five thousand, and they were devoted to the apostles' teaching and fellowship.

And the apostles, with great power, were giving their testimony of the resurrection of the Lord Jesus, supported by the signs before their enemies not with sword or weapon. We must bear witness of them especially and summarize the words of the prophets because the honour of the glorious feast is their duty, for they saw things firsthand and touched them with their hands and ate and drank with Him after His holy resurrection. And as they grieved in His sufferings, so they rejoiced doubly in His resurrection and turned their sorrow into joy as the Lord said to them. And He completed all things for them. Which the prophets desired to see as He said: "Truly I say to you that many righteous prophets desired to see what you have seen and did not see, and to hear what you have heard and did not hear."

Then blessed are their members that were sanctified by it, saying: "But blessed are your eyes because they see, and your ears because they hear."

Truly you have deserved all blessings and joy, O pure apostles, because you have witnessed all the works of the Lord from their beginning to their perfection. Come now among us, O holy evangelists. What are you in our calling today, but we are in your calling, O noble apostles who invited all peoples to the feast of the Lord, as they were commanded after His holy resurrection.

Especially today, we adorn our minds with you, helping each other to praise the honour of the glorious resurrection, for it is not just in your time that you preached it, but your voices remain crying out to eternity!

Here I begin first of all from Matthew, because he mentioned the time of the resurrection itself when the Lord rose by saying: "And there was a great earthquake and the angel of the Lord descended from heaven and rolled away the stone from the door of the tomb and sat on it." The earthquake was at the time of the Lord's resurrection, just as when he gave up His spirit, His voice shook the earth, so also at His resurrection He shook it, to declare that He who died is the one who rose and was not weak. He is the powerful conqueror of death and the master of the general resurrection for all.

The Lord rose, and the stone was sealed on the door of the tomb, just as He was born of the Virgin as prophesied by the prophet Ezekiel, and like His entrance to the disciples with closed doors. For He is able to pass through things without hindrance.

As for the angel rolling the stone away from the tomb's door, it was to clearly announce the resurrection so that it would not remain sealed, leading people to believe that His body was still in the tomb.

He said, "The appearance of the angel was like lightning, and His clothing was white as snow," meaning the beauty of his appearance in the resurrection of His Lord. He said, "From fear, the guards trembled and became like dead men."

As it is written in the Book of Exodus: "The angel of the Lord descended to the camp of the Egyptians and the children of

VI Holy Resurrection

Israel, casting darkness upon Pharaoh and his soldiers, and casting light upon Moses and his people." So did the angel in the resurrection here, he cast great fear upon the guards who were confident in their words, then he gave reassurance and strength to the weak and fearful women, removing their terror and making the guards appear as dead, so as not to grieve the hearts of the holy women who came to the tomb.

Those who came to the tomb were Mary the mother of our Lord, the holy Virgin, and with her Mary from the borders of Magdala. Then the angel addressed the women gently, saying, "Do not be afraid," meaning that you are not like those men who thought they could prevent you from approaching the tomb by their strength. What happened to them was what they deserved. But as for you, you are strong, and you knew that you seek Jesus who was crucified.

The angel did not hesitate to announce to the women that the crucified one is the Lord of all who is seen and unseen.

He said, "He is not here. He has risen as He said." He reminded them of the Lord's words to them all before His suffering, that He was destined to be crucified and rise on the third day. He gave them this word as a sign that was shared between him and them with all the apostles, to lead them to accept his message. And afterwards, he wanted to confirm it to them by sight, so he said to them, "Come and see the place where the Lord was," meaning that even though He was crucified in the flesh, He is the Lord of glory who remains. Here we are preaching before His apostles of His crucifixion, suffering, resurrection, and acknowledge Him as the Lord of angels and all people, as we have preached in the Annunciation and the Nativity. For where the heavenly king is, there his heavenly servants will be. When the women remained amazed and astonished by what had happened, the angel directed them, saying, "Hurry and go, and tell His disciples that He is going ahead of you to Galilee." The angel mentioned Galilee to announce that the Lord had informed him of the things that were between Him and his apostles, and allowed him to announce to those who were ready to spread the message to the whole world, meaning the pure apostles.

St Matthew writes, "So they returned quickly with great fear and joy to inform His disciples." I mean that they believed the angel's words with the signs he had given them.

They believed that the Lord had risen. They hurried in fear of the Jews who were watching the place, but their joy overcame the fear because of the Lord's resurrection.

He said, "When they went to inform his disciples, Jesus appeared to them and said, 'Rejoice.'" I mean that the Lord arranged the situation with them and established them gradually, first with the earthquake and the appearance of the angel to them, and the signs He fulfilled for them. When they believed, they returned to inform His disciples. At that moment, they experienced the appearance of the Lord to them, which is the perfection of realization. He said "So we held His feet and worshiped Him." The Lord said to them, "Do not be afraid, go and tell my brothers to go to Galilee, there they will see me."

When His mother was present, He singled her out for joy to remove Eve's sorrow, and her companion deserved to attend with her because she was concerned about her state and did not let her go alone, but shared in her sorrow and fatigue. Therefore, she deserved to share in the joy with her. He did not prevent them from approaching Him, and offered them His feet to hold and removed their sorrow and fear as well, then He sent them to announce to His holy apostles. And His mother, who was in the house of John the Evangelist to comfort her, became a messenger to him and his friends the apostles to add to her joy!!

VI Holy Resurrection

He also comforted the apostles with His message and called them His brothers to fulfil what was written: "I declare Your name to my brothers," then he reminded them of Galilee, to fulfil His promise to them with a second reminder.

This indicates that Saint Matthew recorded the resurrection before the other evangelists because he mentioned the earthquake, the descent of the angel, how the stone rolled away from the tomb door, and how the guards became like dead men from the fear of His appearance.

The second to record the resurrection is Saint John, because he said "Mary Magdalene came early in the morning" and mentioned that she found the stone rolled away from the tomb door, and did not mention that she found the guards altogether, because when they saw the frightening sight, they got up after effort, as the Lord allowed them and they saw the stone rolled away from the tomb door, and did not find the body of the Lord Jesus so they could not stay due to the abundance of fear that overcame them, but they went to the city and informed the chief priests of what had happened as the Gospel witnesses, and that is why they did not return to the tomb, and the chief priests did not send others, because they realized that the body of the Lord Jesus was not in the tomb but had risen, and that is why when Peter and John came they did not find the guards and likewise the rest of the women who also came to the tomb until sunrise. As for the fact that the Lord left the clothes in the tomb where He rose, this reassures us that in the general resurrection, no one needs clothing or anything used in this world, but they will be like the angels of God in heaven as the Lord witnessed.

The third to record the resurrection is Saint Luke the Evangelist because he mentioned the arrival of the women for the third time close to morning when the light began to appear, when they saw angels resembling men in shining garments like lightning, to also indicate their joy in the resurrection of their Lord. And they said to the women, "Why do you seek the living among the dead?!" Meaning that even though He had suffered and died in the flesh, He remains alive in His divinity, then they said, "He is risen and is not here." They first acknowledged that He is eternally living in His divinity, then they later announced His resurrection from among the dead in His humanity because He is the incarnate God able to do both. The angels reminded them of the words of the Lord who foretold His sufferings and resurrection, and they believed it because these women who followed the Lord from Galilee and from the borders of Magdala who served Him with their wealth, were righteous and holy women. The Lord did not hesitate to appear to them because He saves all of creation, and there is no distinction between man and woman in the Lord, and God only desires our souls to be pure for each of us, whether man or woman, this is what He desired and manifested through our blessed Lady, the Virgin Mary, for the greatness of her purity.

The women, due to their great love for the Lord and their desire for the salvation of their souls, followed Him until the crucifixion, and they did not fear, but stood firm at His cross as the Gospel witnessed. They witnessed everything until the Lord gave up His spirit and was buried, except for His mother whom He entrusted to the Evangelist John, and these women were very dedicated and suffered for Him, crying and mourning for Him.

When evening came, each of them went their separate ways to their acquaintances. Some of them gathered together, while others were alone.

Due to their diligence, early in the morning they arrived at the tomb at different times from the location they were in. Their coming was also different from the angels who informed them,

VI Holy Resurrection

and they deserved the consolation from the angels for their sorrow and love for the Lord, their true commitment to Him, causing non-believing men to weep for them.

The fourth person who recorded the arrival of the women at the tomb was Mark. He said, "They came to the place where the sun had risen" (Mark 16:2), and the evidence that they were not the first women is their statement, "Who will roll away the stone from the door of the tomb for us?" If they were the first and came in another group, they would not have said anything like this.

But if you say to me, Mark mentioned Mary Magdalene along with the group of women!!

I tell you that she is not the one mentioned by John, because everyone without a doubt is from the surrounding area of Magdala, and Mark himself in the chapter following this mentions the one mentioned by John, as he gathered everything mentioned by the other three evangelists in the resurrection account in his chapter by summarizing, saying: "He rose early on the first day of the week," and how well he said it because he used this phrase exclusively unlike the other evangelists, as they mentioned the resurrection but did not specify the time when the Lord rose like Mark did. Although Matthew mentioned the earthquake, he did not specify the time of the resurrection. Mark alone said, "He rose early on the first day of the week," clearly indicating that the Lord rose early on Sunday.

He said, "He appeared first to Mary Magdalene, out of whom He had cast seven demons," and by this Mark singled her out here and confirmed that she was not among those women who came to the place where the sun had risen. Because the Lord allowed the evangelists to mention these words to confirm the resurrection with various testimonies!!

Then he mentioned how He appeared to two other disciples in the field, meaning those mentioned by Luke on the road to Emmaus, then he mentioned how He gathered with the eleven and instructed them to preach to all nations and baptize them. This is what Matthew mentioned, where He appeared to them and instructed them to baptize in the name of the Father, the Son, and the Holy Spirit in the whole world.

As for Luke and John, they mentioned the appearance of the Lord to His disciples on the evening of the resurrection day, and they saw His hands, feet, and side, and ate with Him. Even though after the general resurrection for all there will be no eating or drinking, nor if someone had a wound in His body will he will rise with that wound, nor if he had one eye or was lame or similar will he rise with these physical defects, otherwise where would the absence of corruption be? But the Lord did this to show us all that the body that suffered and died was raised from the dead.

When they thought He was a spirit, He allowed them to touch Him, as He said: "A spirit does not have flesh and bones as you see I have." Just as He confirmed His divinity by the appropriate miracles, He also confirmed His humanity by doing these things and similar ones. He showed his wounds after His resurrection to remove doubts from those who seek doubts!

As for Matthew, He mentioned a strange phrase that we must mention, which is His saying, "on the eve of the Sabbaths, at the dawn, toward the first of the Sabbaths, came Mary." It is known that those seven days are called Sabbaths, as they are with us called Sundays. His saying: "on the eve of the Sabbaths, at the dawn, toward the first of the Sabbaths, came Mary." The women refrained on the Sabbath as in the law, meaning they did not do anything or approach the tomb so as not to give the

VI Holy Resurrection

Jews an excuse. When the Sabbath was over, they were allowed to act as in the law.

Lady Mary went out of natural affection to see the tomb because she did not stay at the cross until the end, and her companion, as mentioned by John, who stood with her at the cross, went out with her. They saw the tomb sealed and the guards sitting, then they returned together to their place, and they returned very early in the morning, at the time of the earthquake, because the lady remembered the Lord's words that He would rise on the third day. She could not bear the intensity of what was in her heart! She was not afraid of the Jews or the guards because of her strong faith in the Lord, and that no harm would come to her. Her companion also went with her to the tomb. That is why the Gospel mentions the events in sequence, first mentioning the evening of Friday when Joseph took the body, then early on Saturday when they sealed the tomb. It mentioned the evening of Saturday when the lady went to see the tomb. Then early on Sunday when she returned to the tomb again. Because she returned twice, in the evening she looked, then in the morning at the time of the resurrection, so Matthew combined the two returns into one context, saying: "on the eve of the Sabbaths, at the dawn, toward the first of the Sabbaths, came Mary..."

John distinguished himself by mentioning the Lord's entry to the disciples with closed doors on the second Sunday of the Resurrection, which is the eighth day of the feast called the Sunday of Sundays or the New Sunday. He allowed the Apostle Thomas to touch him after seeing the marks of the nails and the spear wound. This was not a reproach to Thomas because He understood his beautiful intention, but to be a true messenger proclaiming what he saw firsthand, and Thomas cried out in strong faith saying: "My Lord and my God." The Lord said to him, "Because you have seen me, you have believed; blessed are those who have not seen and yet have believed." By this,

He meant all the people who accept faith in His name. John also mentioned the appearance of the Lord to them on the Sea of Tiberias. He instructed Peter to take good care of all the flock, and He appeared to them for a full forty days after the Resurrection, as witnessed in the Acts of the Apostles. He concealed His divinity from them with the power of His divinity, until their longing for Him grew stronger. Then He appeared to them as He pleased, so that they may be filled with His words and keep them. Perhaps someone may say: How did the Lord appear first to His mother, and here Mark says that He appeared first to Mary Magdalene, from whom He cast out seven demons, but then how does the Apostle Paul say that He appeared first to Peter the Apostle?!

If the inquirer wants to know this well, it is said to him: The apostles are messengers and witnesses for Him to all, both Jews and Gentiles. Mark intended not to take the testimony of relatives in the case of the Resurrection, but of strangers as it is among people. Therefore, He mentioned first Mary Magdalene, then Mary the mother of James, and Salome.

As for Paul, he followed the custom of the law as they did not acknowledge the testimony of women but men. So Peter was mentioned first, who was sought and proclaimed in front of them with power and declaration supported by the deeds and wonders that God performed through him. For the Lord first appeared to His mother before all humans, who in reality represents everyone is the beginning of all joys and the first of delights... Then the first He appeared to from strangers was Mary Magdalene because of her love for the Lord. And the first man He appeared to was Peter the apostle, and we find Luke agreeing with Paul in this when He mentioned the apostles gathered together saying truly the Lord has risen and appeared to Peter. So Paul took the testimony from the men because they were the ones who witnessed His resurrection among all

VI Holy Resurrection

the peoples, and that is why Paul did not mention women at all in the context of the resurrection, neither before nor after. Because he wrote the letters in the form of good news and did not mention women, and the evangelists mentioned the things first and foremost in terms of arrangement, so they mentioned women. Paul said, "And after that, He appeared to the twelve apostles," meaning that Peter was also present with them. He said, "And after them, He appeared to more than five hundred brothers at once," meaning the seventy and the assembly of disciples who followed Him also deserved to see Him. He said, "And after them, He appeared to James, then to the rest of the apostles," meaning all those who sought refuge with them because they were in agreement with the apostles in their love for God and faith in Him. Therefore, they deserved to see Him, and the apostle showed that they were a large group, as he wrote that the Lord distinguished seventy others, meaning he distinguished them from the group as he also distinguished the twelve. St Paul wrote, "And last of all, He appeared to me, the least of all," meaning after the disciples, and He did not preach in vain, but the Lord helped him like all His apostles, and made him a preacher of faith in his name among all the peoples.

I wanted to delve into the words that Paul the apostle put in his letters regarding the resurrection, and how he praised it and honoured it greatly, and how it is the source of eternal life. That through Adam came death, and through the resurrection of Christ, life reigned, and through it hope in the resurrection from the dead for all of us. Just as through Adam came the rule of death, I feared that the explanation would be lengthy and tiresome for the reader and listener alike, and I knew that this in itself does not reach the honour of praising the resurrection of our Lord Jesus Christ from the dead. This is the day on which He rested from all His works on earth, and He blessed the wilderness that was and will be holy on this day, because He sanctified all the days as it is written. Indeed, every firstborn is holy to the Lord among people, animals, and beasts. How much more sanctified is Sunday, which is the first of all that God created on earth, because in it God created all things and then distributed them in the remaining days one by one. Likewise, in it the firstborn also rose in resurrection from the dead.

It is written in the Book of Creation that God rested on the seventh day, and it is known that God did not work with any tools or fatigue until He rested because He willed it to be and it was, as written. And if there was fatigue in creation, then God was not a Creator forever. He sends rain at its appointed time, on the Sabbath and other days. He cares for His creation and sends down dew for the growth of fruits, and He brings forth the wind by His command on the face of the earth, and He provides food for all flesh. And whoever thinks that the world is managed by him and through him after creation is mistaken, because the Prophet says: "The eyes of all look to You, and You give them their food in due season" (Psalm 145:15). And the Lord says: "He makes His sun rise on the evil and on the good, and sends rain on the just and on the unjust." As for the Sabbath, it is the completion of the week, in which the name of rest is mentioned, meaning the renewed rest in the perfection of the world for those who deserve it through Christ.

And as for the Lord, He truly incarnated, suffered, and rose on this holy day, which is the first of days. This is the day that the Lord made special, He who is the firstborn in the resurrection from the dead. He blessed and sanctified it because in it He rested from all His works that He began to do on earth, and He gave rest to all creation that was first as He saved them from Hades, and those who follow He saves them by faith and makes them better than the first. Therefore, we must keep this day and be devoted to reading, praying, and studying the teachings of the Lord as the holy apostles commanded us, saying that God

VI Holy Resurrection

gave us Sunday in place of the Sabbath, so we must keep it more diligently than the Sabbath because in it is the complete rest that is not accompanied by fatigue. Let us be watchful and alert on this night as the laws of the covenant command us, saying: "The night of the Lord's resurrection, so let us be greatly cautious so that no one sleeps in it", then wash your bodies with water before dawn, because at this hour the Saviour made all creatures free, His heavenly and earthly servants. For He rose from the dead and ascended to the heavens and sat at the right hand of the Father, and He will also come in His glory and His angels with Him, and He will reward each one according to his deeds. Those who did good to the resurrection of eternal life and those who did evil to the resurrection of judgment as it is written. Also, in the book of the Didascalia, the teachings of the holy apostles says this: "The Lord rose from the dead, so you also rise among yourselves what we have commanded you by our hands, saying do this in remembrance. Then break your fast while you are rejoicing that the Lord Jesus has risen from the dead, and has become the pledge of our resurrection, and this will be for you an eternal law until the coming of the Lord".

My beloved, we must make this Easter a feast, not with leaven of malice and bitterness, but with the leaven of purity and holiness because with this sacred resurrection we are intended to be born anew from the earth with a resurrection that does not fade. As our teacher Peter says: "Blessed be the God and Father of our Lord Jesus Christ, who according to His abundant mercy has begotten us again to a living hope through the resurrection of Jesus Christ from the dead, to an inheritance incorruptible and undefiled and that does not fade away, reserved in heaven for you" (1 Peter 1:3-4). And the apostle Paul says, "just as Christ was raised from the dead by the glory of the Father, even so we also should walk in newness of life" (Romans 6:4), for because of this noble resurrection all the apostles, prophets, martyrs, and saints hoped for it, and for it they kept the commandments and rejected the glory of this world. Look at the diligence of the perfect man in God, the divine apostle Paul, and how he says: "Not having my own righteousness, which is from the law, but that which is through faith in Christ, the righteousness which is from God by faith; that I may know Him and the power of His resurrection, and the fellowship of His sufferings, being conformed to His death, if, by any means, I may attain to the resurrection from the dead" (Philippians 3:9-11). Look at this noble apostle, how he knew the power of the resurrection of the Lord, that it saves from corruption those who keep it, how he struggled for it, showing that it is the righteousness of perfection that is born from faith in Christ. Let us, the weak, strive so that the bestial desire may die in us now, so that the angelic purity may shine in us. Let us kill our members on earth, which will decay in the dust, so that we may rise to a luminous life and fulfil in us the word of the noble apostle who said: "For if we have been united together in the likeness of His death, certainly we also shall be in the likeness of His resurrection" (Romans 6:5).

Let us reconcile with each other with a brotherly kiss so that we may deserve the peace that the Lord gave to His apostles at His resurrection from the dead, and fill us with His Holy Spirit. Remember the toil of your fasting that has passed, so do not accept for yourselves to fall into sins, and defile your souls and bodies together, but we must rejoice in the resurrection of our Lord, through which we obtain eternal life. If we have love in imitating Him, let us keep ourselves without sin according to our strength. For food does not separate us from God, for everything is pure to the pure in the type of food if taken with moderation, and the mind is preserved from indulging contrary to the commandment.

VI Holy Resurrection

Fifty days our Lord has given us to commemorate His honourable resurrection, and it does not oblige us to physical asceticism. Rather, in it we must preserve the spiritual mind because our feasts are spiritual, not Jewishly physical, so that the One who rose from the dead may delight in us and grant us a share in the resurrection where we don't experience death, nor pain, nor affliction, and we become the children of the Kingdom and the children of the Resurrection as promised to us. So we wash our bodies with water, and as for our souls, we cleanse them with virtuous deeds.

Our homes are illuminated with lamps, and as for the deceitful corners of our hearts, they are illuminated with purity as He handed to us saying: "Take heed therefore that the light which is in you is not darkness" (Luke 11:35). Then He said, if your body is luminous and there is no dark part in it, meaning the parts of the organs, do not be in a dim darkness, for it will be all luminous just as a lamp illuminates for you with the brilliance of its light.

We revive the dead works in order to reach the Resurrection with the One who rose from the dead.

We share with our needy and poor brothers in our abundant table for this feast, so that Christ may share with us in the heavenly invitation. And let it be known that what is in your hand is not yours, but a gift from Him, and by His grace He rewards you with goodness when you do good with your partner in servitude, as it is written: "Give to God what is His, and He will consider it a loan kept with Him."

And we ask our Lord Jesus Christ, who rose from the dead, to strengthen our fallen spirits to care for what pleases Him, and to forgive us for our past sins, and to overlook our faults, and to support us in keeping His commandments for the rest of our lives, and to grant the souls of our deceased who have rested in faith in His holy name, through the intercession of our blessed Lady, the Virgin Mother of Salvation, Saint Mary, and through the intercession of the pure apostles, martyrs, and righteous saints, and all those who have pleased the Lord with their good deeds. Amen.

VII

The Feast of the Ascension

Translated from the arabic edition
by Fr Mancarius Awad

In the name of the Father, and of the Son, and of the Holy Spirit, one God, Amen.

Homily on The Glorious Ascension
By the Honoured Saint Bulus al-Bushi

May his prayers and blessings be with us until the last breath, Amen.

O Christ our God, who ascended to heaven bodily and filled all with His divinity, raise our aspirations from the earthly to the heavenly.

O Lord, who honoured the human race by raising the body taken from them to where the glory of His eternal divinity resides, elevate our minds from the shortcomings of this world to the heights of that renewed eternity.

O Lord God, who exalted earthly beings to become heavenly, accept us to You, O Lord God who is above all authority and power, grant me, O Holy One, to speak of the dignity of Your ascension to the eternal realm in which You have always been.

O Emmanuel our God, who granted the earthly to attain the rank of the heavenly, grant me speech to proclaim the glory of Your marvellous ascension with the body to the heavens where You eternally reside in divinity.

Grant me knowledge, O You who bestowed grace, salvation, and elevation upon our fallen race, raising it up to the everlasting kingdom of heaven, so that I may proclaim Your goodness as You ascend to the heights of Your heavens, and send with David the psalmist and say, "God has gone up with a shout, the Lord with the sound of a trumpet. Sing praises to our God, sing praises, to our King, sing praises. For God is the King of all the earth. Sing praises with understanding. God reigns over the nations. God sits on His holy throne" (Psalm 47).

VII The Feast of the Ascension

I proclaim also with him Your entry into the gates of eternal glory and say: "Lift up your gates, O you princes! And be lifted up, you everlasting doors! And the King of glory shall come in. Who is this King of glory? The Lord of hosts, He is the King of glory" (Psalm 24).

And I tell him of the captivity that You had taken from the hand of the devil by the ascension of the body with which You united and bestowed Your talents upon humans. And I say: "He ascended to the highest and took captivity captive and gave gifts to people" (Eph 4:8). And we bow down to You and praise all together, saying, "O all you kings of the earth, praise the Lord. Sing to the Lord who ascended to the highest heavens in the east", and I also send to You with him a new hymn because the old things have passed away, and everything has been renewed in You, O Christ the Lord who renewed creation with His resurrection and elevated its rank with His ascension. And we all say together, saying with one accord, "Praise the Lord with a new hymn. Praise the Lord, all the earth, bless His name. Proclaim His salvation day after day, declare to the nations that the Lord has reigned (Psalm 96:1, 2), meaning that the devil has been defeated, and the body has obtained eternal kingship as He said to His disciples after His resurrection. "All authority in heaven and on earth has been given to me, and though the authority is His, I mean the body that was given dignity and authority by its union with the divinity and its resurrection from the dead. And thus we understand the nature of the ascension, the sitting, and the kingship, as David said, "The Lord has reigned, let the earth rejoice, clouds and darkness surround Him, righteousness and justice are the foundation of His throne" (Psalm 97:1). This is the kingship that Gabriel the angel announced to the Virgin Mary, saying: "And He will reign over the house of Jacob forever, and His kingdom will have no end." And David also says, "The Lord said to my Lord, 'Sit at my right hand until I make your enemies a footstool under your feet. The Lord will send you a sceptre of power from Zion, and you will rule in the midst of your enemies forever" (Psalm 110:1). And this passage was explained by the Lord in the Gospel, and thus his name, the Holy One, has reigned in the midst of His enemies, not until a time of expiration, but forever without end. And by His enemies, he meant the rebellious demons, the unbelieving Jews, and those who did not submit to faith in His name, as he said, "But those enemies of mine who did not want me to reign over them, bring them here and kill them in front of me" (Luke 19:27), meaning vengeance against them in His second coming. And truly, beloved brothers, the glory of this honourable feast, meaning the feast of the ascension of our Lord Jesus Christ to heaven, is very glorious because in it is the completion of the divine plan with the mystery of incarnation.

Today the Lord ascended to the heavens with His body, and He is there in His divinity, never ceasing, and it is mentioned that He descended, meaning that He incarnated, and it is mentioned He ascended, meaning that He remained with the body with which He united, above all rule and authority.

Today the Lord ascended to the highest heavens, and the angels, rulers, and powers submitted to Him.

Today, He who was once beneath everyone fallen in the dust and afflictions of the earth, is now above all in the heavens. And when humans looked at the body that had fallen into the abyss, and saw that it had risen to the heavens above all that is seen and unseen, they knew that destruction had passed, anger had gone and ended, and the glory of the freedom of sonship had been illuminated by our Lord Jesus Christ. Because how can the earth ascend to the heavens if the Lord of heaven did not unite with it in the wondrous incarnation "and ascended to where His glory is beyond comprehension." And how can the earthly bodies become spiritual if the Lord of spirits did not incarnate from them, the God of all flesh, and restore everything as is fitting. How can the prisoners under the rule of death and decay reach the rank of those who were not subject to the rule of death, namely the angels, if their nature was not united with that righteous conqueror of death and raised above all? For everything is subject under His feet.

Grace did not remain for us because of the offense, but the grace of our Lord Jesus Christ exceeded all offenses and mistakes and reached heights until it reached the heavens above all angels, rulers, and powers.

The prophet Elisha teaches us the secret of His ascension, which is written in the Books of Kings that if the sons of the prophets came to the prophet Elisha and dwelt with him, he said to them, "Brothers, there is not enough room for all of us in this place, so cut wood from the bank of the Jordan River and make yourselves a place to dwell in."

They only had one axe, so they took it and went to cut with it. The axe head flew off the handle and fell into the Jordan River, which was a place of very strong currents. They came and informed the prophet Elisha of this, so he took a new stick other than the first one and came to the place where the axe had fallen and threw the new wood into the river, and the iron floated. The prophet reached out his hand and took the axe, and this was an example of the spirit of prophecy for humanity, which had fallen into the sea of the world and sank like heavy iron and could not ascend. So the heavenly Lord had compassion and united with a pure body that was not tainted by sin, but was taken from the virgin Mary without human seed, then raised it without hindrance as is fitting, and gave our kind the power to ascend to where His glory is, as the apostle says, "Let us hold fast the confession of our hope without wavering, for He who promised is faithful. And let us consider how to stir up one another to love and good works" (Hebrews 6:18). And he also said, "Let us then with confidence draw near to the throne of grace, that we may receive mercy and find grace to help in time of need."

Jacob Israel preceded and saw how the Lord ascended, where he saw a high ladder from the earth to the sky, with angels of God descending and ascending on it, and the Lord above the top of the ladder.

This indicates the providence of the Lord, which He completed with the human incarnation and ascended from one to another like a ladder, from the incarnation to the ascension, with the angels serving Him throughout, from the announcement to the resurrection and ascension.

Come into our midst today, O holy evangelist Luke, so that we may take from you the context of the saying about the ascension of the Lord, and how the Gospel was written with the support of the Spirit from the beginning of the incarnation, completing it with the ascension. Then it also began with the ascension in the book of Acts, making it the opening of the book, then mentioned how the fulfilment of the Gospel was achieved, and combined the two in the ascension. He said, "The first account I composed, Theophilus, about all that Jesus began to do and teach" (Luke 1:1), meaning the policy of the Lord's providence, that He first acted and taught us to follow His footsteps, and in order to show that all He did was for our discipline and instruction, and not out of necessity.

He gave us an example to work and learn, saying, "until the day when He was taken up," meaning that the noble ascension is the perfection of the human Gospel, and in it the saying about the type of God's providence ended, saying, "after He had by the Holy Spirit given orders to the apostles whom He

VII The Feast of the Ascension

had chosen," meaning the commandment he mentioned in the Gospel. He said, "To these He also presented Himself alive after His suffering, by many convincing proofs, appearing to them over a period of forty days and speaking of the things concerning the kingdom of God," meaning that He stayed forty days after the holy resurrection, appearing to them from time to time. Sometimes He appeared to them to gladden their hearts by seeing Him, and sometimes He disappeared by the power of His divinity from them so that they would long for Him and remember what He had commanded them and discuss it among themselves. His saying: "speaking about the kingdom of God," means all His teachings for the kingdom of heaven, to which He ascended in the flesh while still united with His divinity. He said, "And while staying with them, He commanded them not to leave Jerusalem, but to wait for what the Father had promised, which He said, 'you heard of from Me.'"

He promised them to send them the gift of the Spirit, and He and the Father are one in mind and power, and for this reason He said "the promise of the Father", so that He may establish to them the unity of the divinity without division. He said "what you have heard from Me," meaning that they heard it from Him and He and the Father are one as He said to the Jews and also said to Philip, whoever has seen Me has seen the Father. He said "John baptized with water, but you will be baptized with the Holy Spirit," mentioning here the honour of baptism that they are expected to receive with the coming of the Holy Spirit upon them when He gives them the gift of perfection. John introduced baptism but with water, you will baptize with the baptism of the Spirit, and then you will be leaders for all the world in the birth from above. He said "not many days from now" meaning the completion of the fifty, so when they asked him about the earthly kingdom of Israel, He removed this worldly preoccupation from their minds and then informed them that when the Spirit comes upon them, He will fill them with knowledge and they will know everything, Not only that but they will receive a superior power so that they may be witnesses for Him not only in one place, but He said in Jerusalem and Judea and Samaria and to the ends of the earth.

When He completed all these things for them and confirmed with them to wait for the promise that will descend upon them from heaven and be a guide, comforter, and teacher for them, then the Lord God blessed them with all blessings and ascended to heaven before their eyes as they watched Him. Then a cloud took Him up to fulfil what is written "He rode on the clouds and walked on the wings of the wind, (Psalm 104:3) meaning that in the imperceptible air and the uncontrolled winds, He ascended with the power of His divinity without hindrance, as if it had wings serving its Creator. As it is also written "clouds and darkness surround Him. Righteousness and justice are the foundation of His throne, (Psalm 97:2) and it is written "He rode on the cherubim and flew, He flew on the wings of the wind, (Exodus 18:10)

First, it mentioned His riding on the cherubim and then mentioned His flying on the wings of the winds to declare the power of His divinity. He does not need anything from His creation but He ascended the united body with strength to the highest spiritual ranks above all intellectual powers, and when they saw him, they all submitted - the angels, the rulers, and the forces - meaning all the spiritual beings above the heavens. As for the apostles, they remained standing, gazing towards Him as He ascended and they were amazed.

And as they were doing so, two men in shining white clothes stood before them, meaning that angels appeared to them in human form so that they could communicate with them and to show us that the heavenly beings have become one with the

VII The Feast of the Ascension

earthly beings through the Lord who ascended with the united body to heaven. For Luke, in his mention of angels, noted that they appear in human form, as mentioned in the Gospel about the angels who announced to the women with this same example. They said, "Men of Galilee," meaning the apostles from Galilee. They said, "Why do you stand looking up into heaven?" meaning that the ascension of the Lord to heaven is not a strange thing. Then they said, "This Jesus who has been taken up from you into heaven, will come in the same way as you saw Him going into heaven," referring to Jesus the Saviour, as he was named for the sake of the incarnation. They declared to them the dignity of His ascension and confirmed His appearance in His second coming from the heaven he ascended to, as the angels intend to come with Him as the Lord said, "He is coming with His holy angels in glory." Then the pure apostles returned to Jerusalem, rejoicing in what they had seen of the glory and honour for the divine appointed time. Then they entered the holy upper room where they had first gathered with the Lord and he had come to them with the doors closed, like servants remembering the place where they were with their master, waiting in hope for the appointed time, and they were joyful.

Our Lady Mary was also with the devout women who were constantly in prayer and supplications with the apostles with one soul, all waiting for the appointed time of the Holy Spirit, longing for what they had heard from the Lord that in Him is the perfection of knowledge, and He is the guide to truth. For in him they are given the strength to spread the good news throughout all the earth.

Let us now magnify, beloved, the ascension of the Lord Jesus Christ and honour and glorify Him, for through Him our earthly perishable nature has been honoured and elevated to a heavenly status, as the apostle says, "But God, who is rich in mercy, because of His great love with which He loved us, even when we were dead in trespasses, made us alive together with Christ" (Ephesians 2:4).

We prostrate and glorify the one to whom the angels, leaders, and forces have submitted. We go out with His apostles mentally outside the city - which is departing from the sensory world - then we ascend to the mountain, which is the elevation of the mind above vice - to the height of virtue to bless us with His pure and noble chosen ones, and we prostrate to Him with them. Then we recite with the prophet and singer David saying "Exalt the Lord our God and worship at His holy mountain, for the Lord our God is holy" (Psalm 99:9). We also say we enter His tent and prostrate in the place of His holiness, then we ascend to the highest point and stay looking towards Him, hoping for Him to grant us the gift of His Holy Spirit, so that He may guide us to righteousness and truth, as the apostle teaches us by saying "If then you have been raised with Christ, seek the things that are above, where Christ is, seated at the right hand of God. Set your minds on things that are above, not on things that are on earth, for you have died, and your life is hidden with Christ in God" (Colossians 3:1-3). We should not think of the right hand as a physical hand, but rather as a symbol of power and honour, as the body that was once below all is now seated above, and Paul explains this by saying "He has put all things under His feet and has made Him the head over all things for the church, which is His body, the fullness of Him who fills all in all" (Ephesians 1:22-23).

Let us now reject the defilement of the world and seek the honour that has been bestowed upon us, so that we may not be the cause of our own destruction.

Let us keep our bodies pure and our souls pure and bright for the One who united with humanity in love and raised it to the highest heavens.

VII The Feast of the Ascension

Let us make peace with one another for the One who ascended to the heavens and made the earthly and heavenly beings one.

Let us show mercy to the needy for the One who has shown us mercy and has given us everything abundantly for our needs.

Let us walk before Him in a straight path so that we may be worthy of ascending to the heavenly heights, where the head of eternal life has gone before us, the saviour of all creation. Let us love purity and cleanliness and strive to preserve them so that the light of His grace may shine within us in the heights of our souls and fill us with the gift of His Holy Spirit.

We proclaim His glory, speak of His wonders, and declare the power of His salvation, the greatness of His arm. We recite what He has done for us so that we may be worthy of companionship with His holy apostles who proclaimed His name among kings, rulers, and all peoples with diligence and love throughout their lives. For the apostle boasts of this and recites in these words, saying: "Great is the mystery of godliness: God was manifested in the flesh, justified in the Spirit, seen by angels, preached among the Gentiles, believed on in the world, and received up in glory" (1 Timothy 3:16).

And we ask our Lord Jesus Christ, who ascended to the heavens, to lift us up with His power from the sea of this perishing world. To establish our feet in the straight path. To forgive our past deeds. To help us work according to His will and keep His commandments, and to have mercy on all the baptized who have passed away in the hope of faith in His holy name, through the intercession of our blessed Lady, the holy Virgin Mary, the mother of salvation, and all the holy apostles, martyrs, and righteous saints. Amen.

VIII

The Feast of Pentecost

Translated from the arabic edition
by Fr Mancarius Awad

In the name of the Father and of the Son and of the Holy Spirit, one God Amen.

Homily on Pentecost or the Descent of the Holy Spirit
By the honourable Saint Bulus al-Bushi
May his prayers and blessings be with us until our last breath, Amen

O Holy Spirit, proceeding from the Father, the heavenly King, Spirit of truth, present everywhere, filling all things, treasure of good things and giver of life, come and dwell in us, cleanse us from all impurity, O Holy One, and save our souls.

O You who granted students noble wisdom until they became teachers and guides to all mankind, grant, O living Spirit, Your servants a provision that leads to eternal life so that we may live through You.

Raise me, the humble one, to speak of Your dignity, O Spirit of truth, who speaks in souls, prophets, and saints forever.

Give me knowledge, O giver of all excellent talents, so that I may proclaim Your glory equal to the Father and the Son in essence and eternity.

Guide me logically, O One who gave birth to us for the second birth that never fades, for the hope of eternal life, and through You we dare to call upon God our Father, so that I may speak of the majesty of Your dignity and the power of Your actions that exist everywhere.

O Holy Spirit, proceeding from the Father eternally and abiding in the Son eternally, united in one essence without beginning or end.

VIII The Feast of Pentecost

You are the Spirit of life, the Spirit of purity, the Spirit of chastity, the Spirit of strength, the Spirit of many sacred and virtuous talents, the Spirit of preaching, the Spirit of prophecy, the Spirit of holiness, the Spirit of knowledge.

The Spirit of wisdom, the Spirit of steadfastness, the Spirit of patience, the Spirit of faith. The One who works in every authority and power, not as a servant but as a ruler present with everyone, existing everywhere. The One who contains everything but nothing contains Him. The strong who does not object, and the worker in the kingdom, that does not limit the simple in nature, great in actions, mighty in power, the source of noble gifts, the fountain of high talents, the giver of speech to the prophets, preaching to the apostles, encouragement to the martyrs, purity to the virgins, asceticism to the saints, the sanctifier in the rank of priesthood, the father who baptizes children for God, and through Him we complete the sacrifice from the east to the west and from the north to the south.

The Spirit of truth and the Paraclete, the Comforter, who proceeds from the Father, we worship and glorify Him with the Father and the Son, as the Orthodox faith has handed down to us.

And thus we believe that the Holy Trinity is one divinity because God exists, speaking, living forever. So when we say God, we are saying the Father, the Son, and the Holy Spirit, because their essence does not exceed that and does include less than that. And by this we do not worship three gods, lest we be like the pagans who believe in multiple gods. And we are not like the Jews who deny the Word of God and His spirit. Because the error in both is equal, even though their statements are different. Because we argue that God is one with three hypostases and has no equal in this. And this unity has been likened to fire, with heat generated from it and light emanating from it. For the fire is one and the attributes are three for the essence of the one fire, and wherever the flame is found, heat and light are always present with it. Even though the analogy is not the same as the reality in all its aspects, it is intended for one aspect only, because if the analogy does not deviate from the reality in any aspect, then it is the thing itself that is intended by the analogy!! So the Trinity transcends all comparisons for the perfection of its attributes.

If the essence of God Almighty were several individuals, this would imply deficiency and far be it. But because there is no equal to Him, it is necessary to raise Him to perfection, not deficiency. And because He is one essence with three hypostases, His description must rise above all analogies and example, because it is impossible for there to exist in all creation one essence with three hypostases complete in every respect without division in some of its aspects.

This is truly the depiction of God, without adding or detracting, and His depiction has been perfected in one of two ways (i.e., in unity and trinity). As for 'unity', its agreement and suitability in all aspects are described by its essence, while in the three attributes belonging to the personal attributes, they are for the sake of their completeness. Because these attributes are not part of each other, as distancing and division do not suit the content of the whole unless something beyond its essence is reserved for it in a way that exceeds it in power and is manifested in strength, and may God forbid that. So if the matter is like this, it is true that they are complete attributes, showing their perfection in their unity and showing their attributes in their hypostases. And they are complete in their precision, expansion, and containment, one in their essence (with the presence of trinity

VIII The Feast of Pentecost

and unity, for the essence is one), complete in their actions, one theology in their attributes.[1]

And if someone says: Why did you prove that God is a living speaker and that the Word and life are eternal with Him, then you required for every attribute a hypostasis, for He is All-Hearing, All-Knowing and All-Seeing, in the state of eternity and eternity? Then you obligated hypostases for these attributes?! We respond to him by saying that the word and life are only intrinsic attributes, and as for other things, they are actions emanating from the attributes, because the author of the law can only be a speaker, and no one can command and prohibit anyone but one who speaks, and there is no hearer and all-knowing person except one who is living. These and other attributes come from him because they are fabricated by him

Likewise, it is said that He is a Creator through the Word that gives life, as David the Prophet said, "By the word of God I created the heavens, and with the spirit in him all their hosts" (Psalm 33:6). It is also written, "He said, and they were, and he commanded, and they were created" (Psalm 33:9), and the Holy Bible in the Book of Creation says "And God said, 'Let there be light,' and it was so." (Genesis 1:3) And He said, "Let there be light," and it was so. So He created it with His word and gave it life by His Spirit. It is true, then, that the Word and the Spirit are two attributes in themselves from which all the types described by God emanate.

And David the Prophet says: "He sent his word and healed them and delivered them from corruption" (Psalm 107:20)

And about the spirit it says, "You send forth your Spirit, they are created, and you renew the face of the earth" (Psalm 104:30).

---

1 The Arabic in this paragraph is very dense with theological terms (such as خواص , صفة , انواع) and concepts specific to St Bulus Al-Bushi, we've decided to translate it as close to the Arabic as we possibly can.

This is a brief word about the Holy Trinity and about the Word that was a symbol in the books of the prophets, then appeared in the divine incarnation. Then we return to our topic, which is the honour of this glorious feast, meaning the Paraclete, the Comforter, the Spirit of Truth who spoke in the Law and the Prophets, as it is written in the beginning of the book of creation "In the beginning God created the heavens and the earth. The earth was formless and empty, and darkness was over the surface of the deep, and the Spirit of God was hovering over the waters".

And it is also written in the first book, "And God spoke to Noah, saying, 'My Spirit shall not abide in these people'" (Genesis 6:3). And it is also written in the first book, "Pharaoh said to His servants concerning Joseph, son of Jacob, 'Can we find such a man in whom is the Spirit of God?'" (Genesis 41:38). And it is written in the second book, "The Lord spoke to Moses and said to Him, 'See, I have chosen Bezalel son of Uri, son of Hur, of the tribe of Judah, and I have filled him with the Spirit of God, with ability, intelligence, and knowledge in every kind of craft, to devise artistic designs, to work in gold, silver, and bronze, in cutting stones for setting, and in carving wood, to work in every craft'" (Exodus 31:2-5). And it is written in the fourth book, "And God spoke to Moses, saying, 'Gather for me seventy men of the elders of Israel, whom you know to be the elders of the people and officers over them, and bring them to the tent of meeting, and they shall stand there with you. And I will come down and talk with you there. And I will take some of the Spirit that is on you and put it on them, and they shall bear the burden of the people with you'"...

Moses gathered seventy elders of Israel and set them before the Lord, and the Lord came down in a cloud and spoke to him, and took some of the Spirit that was on him and put it on the seventy elders. And when the Spirit rested on them, they prophesied. But they did not do so again. Two men remained

VIII The Feast of Pentecost

in the camp, one named Eldad and the other Medad, and the Spirit rested on them. They were among those registered, but they had not gone out to the tent, and so they prophesied in the camp. And a young man ran and told Moses, "Eldad and Medad are prophesying in the camp." And Joshua the son of Nun, the assistant of Moses from his youth, said, "My lord Moses, stop them." But Moses said to him, "Are you jealous for my sake? Would that all the Lord's people were prophets, that the Lord would put his Spirit on them!" (Numbers 11:29).

And it is also written in the end of the fifth book, after the death of Moses, that Joshua the son of Nun was full of the spirit of wisdom, for Moses had laid his hands on him. So the people of Israel obeyed him and did as the Lord had commanded Moses (Deuteronomy 9:34).

And it is written that the prophet Samuel had the Spirit of God upon him, and he led the people well, and God was with him and watched over the people all the days of Samuel's life. And when Samuel anointed Saul the son of Kish as king, he said to him, "This is the sign that the Lord has anointed you to be prince over his heritage. When you depart from me today, you will meet a group of prophets coming down from the high place with harp, tambourine, flute, and lyre before them, prophesying. Then the Spirit of the Lord will rush upon you, and you will prophesy with them and be turned into another man" (1 Samuel 10:6), for this is the one Spirit active in prophecy, kingship, and priesthood.

When Samuel anointed David son of Jesse as king and laid hands on him and prayed for him, the Holy Spirit came upon him and he began to prophesy and started to say the Psalms from that day (1 Samuel 16:13). And the Spirit of God was taken away from King Saul when he disobeyed the word of God and did not act upon it (1 Samuel 14:16). Because of this Spirit,

David would plead to God when he sinned, asking for renewal through repentance so that he would not suffer the same fate as Saul. He repented with strength and returned with a noble return, saying, "Create in me a pure heart, O God, and renew a steadfast spirit within me. Do not cast me from your presence or take your Holy Spirit from me. Restore to me the joy of your salvation and grant me a willing spirit, to sustain me" (Psalm 51:10). He also said, "Your good Spirit will guide me on level ground" (Psalm 143:10). And he said further for the Spirit, "I opened my mouth and panted, for I longed for your commandments" (Psalm 119:131).

Isaiah says, "From the beginning, I did not speak in secret; at the time it happens, I am there" (Isaiah 48:16). And he said, "The Spirit of the Lord will rest on him—the Spirit of wisdom and understanding, the Spirit of counsel and might, the Spirit of knowledge and the fear of the Lord" (Isaiah 11:2). He also said, "The Spirit of the Lord is on me, because he has anointed me to proclaim good news to the poor" (Isaiah 61:1). And he said, "My covenant with them is that my Spirit who is on you and my words that I have put in your mouth will not depart from your mouth" (Isaiah 59:21). He also said in Isaiah concerning the Jews, "They have vexed me with their sins and angered the Holy Spirit within them."

Ezekiel says, "The Lord took hold of me, and I was carried away by the Spirit of the Lord to a valley filled with bones. He said to me, 'Prophesy to these bones and say to them, 'Dry bones, hear the word of the Lord!''" (Ezekiel 37:4). Ezekiel also said, "The Spirit of the Lord came powerfully upon me and He said, 'This is what the Lord says'" (Ezekiel 11:5). He also said, "I will sprinkle clean water on you, and you will be clean; I will give you a new heart and put a new spirit in you; I will remove from you your heart of stone and give you a heart of flesh. And I will

VIII The Feast of Pentecost

put my Spirit in you and move you to follow my decrees and be careful to keep my laws" (Ezekiel 36:25, 26).

The Lord said in Daniel, "It is written that the Holy Spirit of God came upon a young man named Daniel" (Daniel 13:45). And Daniel, speaking to King Nebuchadnezzar of Babylon, said, "The wise men of Babylon do not have the Spirit of God in them, so they do not know the unseen and cannot interpret the dreams that I have seen, Your Majesty" (Daniel 2:27, 28).

And it is also written, "Now when the sons of the prophets who were at Jericho saw him opposite them, they said, 'The spirit of Elijah rests on Elisha.' And they came to meet him and bowed to the ground before him." (2 Kings 2:15). How can this be explained when Elijah is greater than Elisha to this day?! Know then that the Scripture did not say anything in vain, but rather the spirit was doubled in the action of the miracles. This is because Elijah performed seven famous miracles, while Elisha performed fourteen well-known miracles!! Elijah raised one dead person through his prayers, and Elisha raised two. However, the action of miracles is not as the prophet wills, but as the spirit who acts in it wills.

And the prophet Micah said, "But as for me, I am filled with power, with the Spirit of the Lord." (Micah 3:8).

And the prophet Haggai said, "For thus says the Lord of hosts: Yet once more, in a little while, I will shake the heavens and the earth and the sea and the dry land." (Haggai 2:6).

And God said in Zechariah, "Thus says the Lord of hosts: Render true judgments, show kindness and mercy to one another, do not oppress the widow, the fatherless, the sojourner, or the poor, and let none of you devise evil against another in your heart." (Zechariah 7:9-10).

I intended to elaborate on the work of the Holy Spirit as mentioned in the prophets, but I feared prolonging the discussion. This Spirit, from whom all noble talents are given, as the Apostle Peter said, "For no prophecy was ever produced by the will of man, but men spoke from God as they were carried along by the Holy Spirit." (2 Peter 1:21).

Let us now summarize the mention of the prophets and talk about the work of the Holy Spirit with the pure apostles, and explain the difference between them and the prophets. For the prophets spoke when the Spirit came upon them as intended, while the apostles had the Spirit dwelling in them constantly, as they were entrusted with the administration of the entire world through the evangelical message, teaching, building, laying hands on leadership, and performing miracles, as the Lord testified to them, saying: "And I will ask the Father, and he will give you another Helper, to be with you forever, even the Spirit of truth, whom the world cannot receive, because it neither sees him nor knows him. You know him, for he dwells with you and will be in you." (John 14:16) Indeed, he remained with them until the end.

They were granted leadership and power superior to the prophets, as the Apostle Paul testified, saying: "And not only the creation, but we ourselves, who have the firstfruits of the Spirit." (Romans 8:23). This means that God honoured the apostles above all ranks, as he said, "He who is the blessed and only Sovereign, the King of kings and Lord of lords, who alone has immortality, who dwells in unapproachable light, whom no one has ever seen or can see. To him be honour and eternal dominion. Amen." (1 Timothy 6:15).

Therefore, no one can see the Holy Spirit as the Lord said: "The wind blows where it wishes, and you hear its sound, but you do not know where it comes from or where it goes" (John 3:8).

VIII The Feast of Pentecost

The apostles were chosen as it is written, "But when he who had set me apart before I was born, and who called me by his grace, was pleased to reveal his Son to me, in order that I might preach him among the Gentiles" (Galatians 1:15).

And the Lord said to Ananias about Paul the apostle, "Go, for he is a chosen instrument of mine to carry my name before the Gentiles and kings and the children of Israel" (Acts 9:15).

And it is written in the book of Acts, "While they were worshiping the Lord and fasting, the Holy Spirit said, 'Set apart for me Barnabas and Saul for the work to which I have called them'" (Acts 13:2).

The Father also called the people, as the apostle says, "For truly, God is faithful, by whom you were called into the fellowship of his Son, Jesus Christ our Lord" (2 Thessalonians 2:14), and he said, "You also are called to belong to Jesus Christ" (Romans 1:6).

And the Lord of glory said, "No one knows the Father except the Son and no one knows the Son except the Father, and anyone to whom the Son chooses to reveal him" (Matthew 11:27).

He said about the Spirit, "When that one comes, He will testify on My behalf and inform you openly on behalf of the Father", and the apostle says, "For who among people knows the things of a person except the spirit of the person within him. In the same way, no one knows the things of God except the Spirit of God, (1 Corinthians 2:11), and he also said, "The Spirit searches everything, even the depths of God" (1 Corinthians 2:10), and He, the Most High, examines the hearts and minds as it is written, and likewise the Son does not need anyone to testify about him to a person because he knows what is in a person, and the apostle says that the word of God is living and active and sharper than any double-edged sword, penetrating to the division of soul and spirit, joints and marrow, discerning the thoughts and intentions of the heart, and nothing is hidden from His sight. Everything is naked and exposed before the eyes of Him to whom we must give account" (Hebrews 4:12), and the Holy Spirit examines the hearts and minds as the apostle says, "But we have the mind of Christ because the Spirit searches everything, even the depths of God" (1 Corinthians 2:10), and the Lord says about Him, "He will take what is mine and declare it to you" (John 16:15), and the Lord says, "Every plant that my heavenly Father has not planted will be pulled up" (Matthew 15:3), and He also said, "No one can come to me unless the Father who sent Me draws them" (John 6:44) and He also said, "Whatever the Father gives me will come to me, and whoever comes to me I will never drive away" (John 6:37), and He said: "Father, those you gave me I have kept, and none of them is lost except the son of destruction" (John 17:12), and He said to Peter: "Flesh and blood has not revealed this to you, but my Father in heaven" (Matthew 16:17), and He said about himself, "I am the way, the truth, and the life. No one can come to the Father except through Me" (John 14:6), and the apostle says, "But now in Christ Jesus you who once were far away have been brought near by the blood of Christ" (Ephesians 2:13), and he said, "For he himself is our peace, who has made the two groups one and has destroyed the barrier, the dividing wall of hostility" (Ephesians 2:14).

For the sake of the Spirit, the Lord says, "When the Spirit of truth comes, He will guide you into all the truth" (John 16:13), and the apostle says, "No one can say 'Jesus is Lord' except by the Holy Spirit" (1 Corinthians 12:3), and he said, "And these things that he speaks are not teachings of human words but teachings of the Spirit" and he said, "You are not of the flesh but of the Spirit".

VIII The Feast of Pentecost

Here we learn the equality of the Holy Trinity, the Father who begot the Son without beginning, and from whom the Spirit eternally proceeds, remaining forever without end. He is the one who speaks of the Father, taking what belongs to the Son, guiding to the truth, speaking in the law, the prophets, the apostles, and the saints. Generation after generation without ceasing. He establishes a complete spiritual law, teaching the apostles, enlightening with the gospel, renewing in the pure a new creation. He gives grace and power without measure. The one who acts in every place and every time. He grants prayer to the praying and blessing to the saints, who is the eloquence of the pure apostles in preaching with the good news until their words reach all the earth, and their voices are heard in the corners of the world in a short period of time. The mighty kings, the powerful governors, the wise, the philosophers, the simple, and the ignorant submitted to them, giving them strength and assistance, as it is written, "God gives the word of the gospel with great power." It is also written, "I will speak your testimonies before kings and not be ashamed," and also written, "I have proclaimed your righteousness in a great assembly and have not restrained my lips." It is also said of them, "Their voice has gone out into all the earth, and their words to the ends of the world" (Psalm 19:4).

Those are truly the rivers of life flowing out of Jerusalem who watered the whole earth as Ezekiel prophesied. Beautiful are they in their warning of the promised blessings, as Isaiah the prophet said, "How beautiful are the feet of those who bring good news." The sweet springs that Moses told us about, the first of the prophets, saying that when they crossed the sea they would come upon twelve springs of water and seventy palm trees (Exodus 27:15), a prophecy about the twelve apostles and the seventy disciples from whom the world received spiritual teachings. They are the knights of the Lord God and His chariot, who carried His holy name in the corners of the earth. The justified soldiers of the heavenly king who fought vigorously against the enemies of their Lord and demolished every false doctrine, and tore down the strongholds fortified by demons in the souls of men. They rejected every frivolous opinion and embraced it in order to know Christ. The chosen messengers of the Lord who were sent to invite the invited to the heavenly wedding. His virtuous servants who served diligently in the Christian community. The people of His household who are knowledgeable of His hidden mystery. The salt of the earth and the light of the world who illuminated our deepest darkness and guided us to the light of guidance... The leaders of all the nations who were born at the beginning of the gospel... The shepherds who were entrusted with the spiritual flock... The steadfast rocks on which Christ laid the foundation of His church. The engineers of the solid harbor for the covenant as the apostle testified, saying: "I laid a foundation, and another builds on it. But let each one take care how he builds on it, for no one can lay a foundation other than that which is laid, which is Jesus Christ" (1 Corinthians 3:10).

They are as farmers because they have cultivated the land of our hearts and planted in it the divine seed. They are as waterers of Christ the King because they have watered our souls from the spring of the Holy Spirit. They are as vine-dressers because they have laboured and worked in the vineyard of our souls. They are as matchmakers because they have betrothed our souls pure to the heavenly bridegroom Christ as the apostle says, "For I feel a divine jealousy for you, since I betrothed you to one husband, to present you as a pure virgin to Christ" (2 Corinthians 11:2). They are intercessors for us before Christ as the apostle says, "We are ambassadors for Christ." They are the ones who gave life to humans in the proclamation of faith, the sacrament of baptism, the laying on of hands for ordination, and the reception

VIII The Feast of Pentecost

of the holy mysteries. In summary, we find them complete in embodying various virtues and talents.

They are messengers and prophets, leaders and teachers of the covenant, martyrs and saints, and all the virtues and talents scattered among the people are found gathered in them so that they do not miss any of the virtues, and no one among humans surpasses them. For thus the Lord God has ordained that those who proclaim His name should not be philosophers from the wise of this world. For if they were so, their words would contradict each other. Just as we find the words of philosophers one by one refuting the words of the other and belittling and exalting themselves over each other. This is because their wisdom is not from God, and if faith were in the wisdom and planning of people, it would be of no use or benefit, for Peter the apostle teaches us in this sense, saying: "For we did not follow cleverly devised myths when we made known to you the power and coming of our Lord Jesus Christ" (2 Peter 1:16).

And the apostle Paul, who was skilled in the law, writes saying, "And I, when I came to you, brothers, did not come proclaiming to you the testimony of God with lofty speech or wisdom. For I decided to know nothing among you except Jesus Christ and him crucified" (1 Corinthians 2:1-2).

Furthermore, if the preaching of the apostles had been supported by the power of the sword and the authority of terror to force people into faith, whether they wanted it or not, it would have been similar to the worship of idols that arose by the sword since about three thousand years after the flood until the coming of our Lord Jesus Christ. Rather, we find the pure martyrs, who were martyred and had their necks struck while remaining patient and steadfast in the faith of our Lord Jesus Christ.

God chose his apostles from among the unlearned and weak, with no understanding of anything in this existence, and He strengthened them and supported them with the gift of the Holy Spirit, conquering the philosophers through them until they submitted to them, and overcoming the power of kings and rulers, the sword bearers, until they yielded to their preaching. That is why the apostle says, "But we have this treasure in jars of clay, to show that the surpassing power belongs to God and not to us." For this light of faith is a true grace from the Spirit, and he gave Him the title the Spirit of the Father or the Holy Spirit because they are one in divinity. As the apostle Paul says: "If the Spirit of God does not dwell in you, you are not of Him, for if the Spirit of Christ does not dwell in a person, he is not of God."

And Peter says, "The salvation that the prophets sought and searched diligently for, proclaiming the Spirit of Christ within them, and testifying in advance to the sufferings of Christ and the glories that would follow" (1 Peter 1:10, 11). It is this one Spirit speaking in the law, the prophets, the apostles, and all the saints forever.

Let us celebrate this feast now with spiritual joy as befits it, so that we may deserve the gift of the Spirit along with the pure apostles, and let us consider how the virtuous and perfect apostles, who had no law left because their deeds were above the law, nevertheless honoured the divine feasts well. The Apostle Paul wrote to the people of Corinth (1 Corinthians 16: 8, 7) saying, "I will remain in Ephesus until the Feast of Pentecost," meaning this honourable feast. He was not willing to move to another place until he celebrated it as befits it. St. Luke wrote in the Book of Acts, when Paul came to the island of Corus proclaiming the good news. He said, "The apostle was diligent in crossing Ephesus so as not to delay in Asia, because he wanted to work on the Feast of Pentecost in Jerusalem" (Acts 20:16).

Consider all the concerns and hardships of the preaching service that the apostle had to endure, and despite all this, he was

VIII The Feast of Pentecost

diligent in honouring the honourable divine feasts because he knew of their dignity. How much more should we care for them with purity of heart so that we may be sanctified by their good remembrance? Because some of those indwelt by the Spirit said, "Just as the king bestows his gifts on royal occasions, wedding days, and seasons on his elite, so God bestows His spiritual gifts on His children who carry out His commandments on the honourable divine holidays."

So we must celebrate now with spiritual purity, in accordance with the Spirit, on the feast of the coming of the Comforter Spirit, so that He may dwell in us, and purify us from our filth. Let us keep the body pure because it is God's temple for the Holy Spirit to dwell in us. Let us keep the soul and all senses pure so that our souls may join the Holy Spirit, and deserve the inheritance of sonship in the eternal kingdom.

The Apostle teaches us such teachings, saying: "Let us now live in the Spirit in agreement with our conscience," and we are careful not to do otherwise, lest the Holy Spirit be displeased. He says, "Do not displease the Spirit of God, by whom you were sealed for the day of deliverance, but let all murmuring and slander be removed from you along with the rest of the evils."

Let us show mercy to the poor so that we may complete the guidance of the soul, for they deserve mercy as mercy is glorified in judgment, as the Apostle Jacob says. Let us make peace and reconciliation with our brothers so that the Spirit may make peace and reconciliation in our struggling souls with the pains of our bodies. Let us comfort the distressed and the imprisoned with our absence so that the Comforter, the Holy Spirit, may strengthen us in our hardships, for it is written, "My spirit will rest on you with a word that will support you with the strong right hand." Let us emulate the spiritual journey of the noble fathers who walked in the Spirit and resemble them so that we may have an inheritance and a share with them in the eternal abodes.

And we ask our Lord Jesus Christ who visited us with mercy and compassion from on high, the Holy One, to renew in us the gift of the Spirit and to purify our souls, and to forgive us our sins, and to overlook our transgressions and forgive us our faults, and to grant us a spiritual journey for the rest of our days, and to rest the souls of our departed ones from all the children of baptism who have fallen asleep in the hope of faith in His holy name.

And make us worthy to hear His joyful voice saying, "Come, O blessed of My Father, inherit the kingdom prepared for you from the foundation of the world… through the intercession of our pure Lady, the Virgin Saint Mary, and the intercession of the pure apostles and all the martyrs and righteous saints. Amen.

www.ingramcontent.com/pod-product-compliance
Lightning Source LLC
Chambersburg PA
CBHW022128080426
42734CB00006B/274